My Greenwich Village
and the
Italian American Community

Carol Bonomo Albright

PublishAmerica
Baltimore

First printing

PublishAmerica has allowed this work to remain exactly as the author intended, verbatim, without editorial input.

ISBN: 1-60836-037-7
PUBLISHED BY PUBLISHAMERICA, LLLP
www.publishamerica.com
Baltimore

Printed in the United States of America

To my son Ed and my daughter Sally
for all the joy they have given me

Introduction

My memories of Greenwich Village are inextricably connected to specific streets, buildings, parks and events in my life. To the light falling on the gray buildings. To the smells that straggled out of its food stores. To the mournful sounds of the foghorn from Battery Park that I could hear at night and the clop of police horses' hoofs on the cobblestones. In this memoir, I've tried first to paint a picture of the Greenwich Village I knew in the 1940s and 1950s—its inhabitants, the buildings we all passed every day, our reactions to them as one group of Villagers, the Italian Americans, and finally the world I inhabited in the summertime.

I've also written about some specific events in my life that occurred in those milieus.* These events could have occurred anywhere, but my reactions to them would have been different. My reactions were colored by my living in a particular place at a particular time with my specific family, descendents of Italian immigrants. Very little, if anything, has been written about Italian Americans' personal experiences in this very special area of New York

City. In an age that values cultural diversity, I think that even those who aren't Italian American will find my story interesting.

Finally, the remembering and writing caused me to imagine my grandmother's life in Italy in the late nineteenth century in order to connect with her in a way that I couldn't do while she was alive. Her life as she lived it will always remain a mystery to me, but I've tried to present some authentic myths about being an Italian *contadina* (peasant) of that time. I use the word 'myth' in the sense not of being something made-up and untrue, but of something which, while made-up, illuminates some deeper truths about a culture.

*To protect the privacy of some individuals, a few names have been changed and one composite character is introduced.

Prologue

Born on Bleecker Street in the late thirties, I grew up in Greenwich Village accepting the diversity that characterized my neighborhood. But some adults were not so sanguine about this jumble of different people living together. The Village was an amorphous set of amoeba-shaped hamlets, expanding and contracting according to the whims or needs of its inhabitants. The Catholic jumble constituted a triangle of oppositions with St. Joseph Church on Sixth Avenue, Our Lady of Pompcii on Bleecker Street, and St.Anthony of Padua Church on Sullivan.

St. Joseph was where Irish and Italian rivalries still persisted beyond their time of intense competition for jobs and their differing ways of practicing their religion. But an internecine rivalry of northern and southern Italians continued between Pompeii and St. Anthony of Padua, each church reversing Italian geography. Pompeii (so southern a location in Italy) was the church where northern Italians worshipped. The southerners, aware of where they weren't wanted, built their own church, St. Anthony of Padua (named for a saint from a northern

Italian city). This was my family's parish.

Added to these oppositions, the Italians lived in a jealous peace south of Washington Square Park with the artists and bohemians who both scandalized and awed them with their prodigal ways. Radicals and the Communist parents of the children attending the Little Red School House, known for its progressive educational ideas, were scattered around Sheridan Square and its environs, mingling with the Italians but really unknown by them.

New York University, lining the west side of Washington Square Park, was inching its way south and squeezing the Italian neighborhood to which Judson House had ministered earlier in the century. Though my mother admired the students who attended NYU—she, who had only an eighth grade education, revered college graduates—she was also wary of them because that very education made them view the world differently from her. Finally professionals of all persuasions and nationalities, as well as those Italian Americans, who had moved out of their original immigrant neighborhood to the larger entity of the Village, lived to the north and east of the park.

As for the fairies, as they were then called, the Italians pitied the homosexuals who lived in the Village because they couldn't have children. Children were the raison d'être for Italians. The few blacks—often tall, muscular men—in the neighborhood could be seen hanging around Sixth Avenue playing basketball in the postage-stamp sized park across from the Waverly theater, in the company of white women. Most Italians wondered about the wisdom of this pairing.

This was the community into which I was born, and from which I would begin to see a larger world.

Chapter 1

South of Washington Sq.:

The Little Red School House

From the beginning of the twentieth century Communists, such as Max Eastman, resided in Greenwich Village. They lived in other New York City neighborhoods too: forty per cent of the Communist Party's American members lived in New York City. But the communists who lived in Greenwich Village were different in that many of the communists in the Village were well known, often writers and artists, like novelist Richard Wright. And then too, they resided there in large enough numbers to have what would today be called a 'support' group. And they could, for the most part, live in Greenwich Village undisturbed—so much so that they even had their own school. Or at least that's what the Italian Americans and the Irish Catholics thought.

Their school was called the Little Red School House, not to reflect the school's political beliefs but rather due to the color of the original building. The word 'red' may well have been what led the Italians and the Irish to believe that this school was communist in orientation—and to some extent they were correct. A sizable number of children of communists attended the school, and its curriculum tended to focus on the oppressed. The oppressed for the Little Red School House were people of color and the workers of the world. While Catholic schools also focused on the oppressed, the oppressed for Catholics were not only the poor, but themselves—discriminated against for being Catholic in America and originally from poor backgrounds. The nuns reminded Catholic students of all the persecutions that Catholics had suffered for their faith from the time of ancient Rome through Poland's Cardinal Midzensky, a modern-day 'martyr' to the Communist regime in his homeland.

Growing up, I passed the Little Red School House almost every day. Though unassuming in looks with its ordinary brick façade, the school loomed large in the imagination of Italian and Catholic Villagers. Elizabeth Irwin founded it in 1922 at P.S 61, fostering progressive education—a fact that in itself would make it suspect among Catholics who distrusted John Dewey and his educational philosophy. Their fear of Dewey was based on his belief that human beings and animals were not different in kind, but in degree. Catholics believed in an evolution in which God at the moment of conception created a human soul for each individual, thus distinguishing human beings from animals.

But if someone with a background similar to theirs practiced Dewey's philosophy—that was another matter. At the other end of New York City in the Bronx, Angelo Patri, son of an Italian immigrant brought up in Italian Harlem, was putting Dewey's philosophy into practice as a principal in two slum schools. Like the founder of the Little Red School House, Patri too had to fight the bureaucracy of the New York City Board of Education. He was more successful than Irwin in staying within the public school system: he practiced progressive education with its emphasis on child-centered schooling from 1907 until 1943 when he retired.

Elisabeth Irwin's Little Red School House maintained the support of the New York City Board of Education for only ten years. When the Board of Education withdrew its support in 1932, the school moved from its 16th Street location to its present one at 196 Bleecker Street in Greenwich Village. The building was perfect for the school because twelve years earlier it had been a settlement house and church, the Church of the Gospel, founded by the First Presbyterian Church of Fifth Avenue to serve the Italian immigrants who populated the area south of Washington Square. The mission lasted only until 1930, freeing the use of the building with its gym, auditorium, classrooms and nursery for the Little Red School House. Later the school bought the old row houses at 200 and 202 Bleecker Street just down the block from the original mission site. Around the corner on Sixth Avenue—as any born New Yorker of a certain age refers to the Avenue of the Americas—and now backing the original school, is Elizabeth Irwin High School, followed by the Bar Pitti, Da Silvanno Restaurant, and the William Passani Ballfield, all concrete, while across the street is a Psychic Advisor—perhaps now patronized by New Age practitioners instead of the Italian immigrants who used to ask for advice from their own fortune tellers.

The 1925 city census shows Bleecker Street housing parents born in Italy with their American-born children, such as Louis Ciano, a retired barber who had arrived in America in 1878 and lived at 200 with his American-born sons James and Frederick. They both became physicians. We do not know if the whole family worked to put the two brothers through medical school, as the immigrants often did. It seems likely despite a barber's occupation being rather lucrative at a time before Gillette Safety Razors. Men relied on a barber's services not only to cut their hair but also to shave them regularly. Nonetheless, a barber would be hard pressed to come up with professional school tuition for two sons.

The elder Ciano's background couldn't have been more different from that of Elizabeth Irwin, the founder of the Little Red School House. Irwin was educated at Smith. Her philosophy put children at the center of their education. She emphasized learning by doing so that field trips were the mainstay of the first two elementary years to the exclusion of traditional academic work. She also stressed that knowledge was not the be all and end all of education, but rather that children needed to inquire, understand and learn how to make their own decisions about their lives.

This last aspect, if the Italian immigrants had known of it, would have led to great consternation. Italian immigrants valued obedience in their children for three reasons: first so that they could control their actions, secondly so that they would make decisions that were best for the family as a whole and thirdly because they thought that their economic future depended upon their children performing their employers' wishes without question. The Board of Education had somewhat similar reservations about Irwin's school. It felt that the school with its highly individualized approach and no formal academic work for the first year and a half didn't fit a child for living in a community. Parents wanted their seven-year olds to be able to read street signs and to count money and get correct change.

Although the school was thought of as 'red,' it coexisted peacefully with the Italian population which generally had a 'live and let live' attitude towards the diversity represented in the Village. While judgments might be made about people different from themselves, the Italians, as well as the other Villagers, rarely took action against each other.

Caroline Ware's book, *Greenwich Village*, published in

1935, is worth reading for her insights into the different value systems of the Italians and the bohemians and professionals who began to re-locate to the Village in the nineteen twenties. She writes that one misunderstanding concerned the spending of money. Having little or no discretionary income, Italians were careful in their spending habits and habitually looked for bargains. Those who weren't Italian, the Americans, as Italian Americans referred to them, had no such tendency since, to them, rents were low and another dollar or two for food or drink wasn't important. They cared most about spending money on cultural events. When buying food, the bohemians never bargained and barely looked at the produce—traits some Italian storeowners used to their own advantage, giving the Americans the wilted head of lettuce, something an Italian woman would never accept.

Moreover, the Italians, whose children were their reason for living, couldn't understand the Americans having no children or only one or two. They viewed this as selfish while the Americans thought that the Italians should have no more children than they could afford.

The Italians also feared that the influx of Americans, richer than they, would cause rents to rise. The Americans wanted apartments with enough bedrooms so that each child could have his or her own room while sharing a bedroom among Italian children was common. The noise children made playing on the street instead of playing in their homes, due to small apartments, annoyed the

Americans while the Italians, who had to get up early to work, were annoyed by the noise the Americans made in the street when exiting parties after midnight. Noise was one situation in which each group acted, calling the police after numerous such events in an effort to have quiet at the time each group wanted. But on the whole the two groups lived side by side without too much discord.

Chapter 2

About Greenwich Village

Washington Square

Washington Square Park in Greenwich Village acted as my playground. Situated at the southern most end of Fifth Avenue, it had been a public park since the early 1800s and its Memorial Arch, designed by McKim, Mead and White, celebrated the centenary of George Washington's inauguration. I played on the swings or the monkey bars in the pocket children's spaces within the larger park, which was open and spacious, yet not so big as to be overwhelming. It was my paradise even when we kids split open the pods of itching powder fallen from the trees and threw them down each other's backs while giving a good rub. Low half-hooped metal fencing reminded us to keep off the grass, an edict we usually obeyed because we appreciated this green oasis in our concrete neighborhood. But we didn't keep off the fence: we practiced 'tight-rope' walking on it, arms extended out on either side to help us balance. The buildings around the park were not very tall, no more than six stories, just like most of the buildings in the neighborhood, thus giving this area of New York City a village feel.

A small space contained a variety of vistas. The arch—originally wood, now stone—was majestic; yet it was not so imposing as to be untouchable. That was where the boys from a number of different neighborhoods—boys from St. Joseph Academy School along with the tougher Irish boys from 16th Street and the Italian boys from south of the park—played stickball after school. We girls watched from a distance—we never met girls from other neighborhoods since girls rarely wandered far from home—while jumping rope or marring the asphalt with chalk marks for a game of hopscotch. We would also wander over to the large fountain, quiet and shut down after the summer heat, and sit along its curved gray wall to talk.

We'd amble over to the southwest section where the checker and chess players—a motley group of older men in rumpled clothes—hung out. Perhaps some of these men were those the nuns warned us about. Our eighth grade teacher advised us not to drink from the water fountains spaced about the park because she said she'd seen men in the early morning hours shaving there. Though shaving in cold water didn't seem possible, we were aware that men from the Bowery—in other words, drunks—made their way uptown to our park and so perhaps it was best to avoid the drinking fountains, though when it was hot, we never did.

We'd also stroll over to the area where the bust of Garibaldi, the military hero of Italy's unification in 1861, stood watch. This statue was installed in 1888. The sculptor, Giovanni Turini, was born in Verona in 1841 and studied in Milan and Rome. He was an appropriate choice to make the bust for he had been a volunteer in the 4th Regiment of Garibaldi's army during the war with Austria in 1866. A year later, Turini settled in New York City where Garibaldi himself had lived in the early 1850s when he was in exile. In 1882, Turini exhibited a group of statuary at the Paris World's Fair.

Italian immigrants who began to populate the area in the last quarter of the nineteenth century had Garibaldi's statue erected. They had first come in small numbers mainly from the north of Italy, but then increasingly from the South. Among them were such people as the artist Joseph Stella whose older brother, a doctor, had arrived in the 1890s. From a middle-class family in the Abruzzi, Joseph was supposed to be a doctor as well. After a year's study, he switched to pharmacy school and finally begged his parents, still in Italy, to send him to art school. His brother had an artist evaluate Joseph's early work. When the artist gave his approval, Joseph was allowed to study art. Dr. Stella, with access to many immigrants like himself who had done well in America, underwrote Joseph's first exhibition at the Tiro A Segno Club.

In the late nineteenth century, wealthy Americans

founded hunting and fishing clubs, which were natural organizations for affluent immigrants to imitate, as many of them had come from rural backgrounds in Italy where hunting and fishing were common. The Tiro A Segno Club also acted as a place for prominent Italians to meet in what was then one of the best dining rooms in New York City. The Tiro A Segno Club is still on MacDougal Street below Bleecker.

Some of Joseph Stella's first sketches were a series of drawings—psychological studies really—of Italian and other immigrants living in the area. Later on he painted the famous Brooklyn Bridge series and the *Madonna of Coney Island* with their emphasis on the movement, light and dynamism of America. Like many an immigrant, he was taken with industrialism and its machines and the sense of new possibilities they brought to the century. Yet he also felt the strong pull of his Italian roots. Towards the end of his life, he returned to these roots and did detailed baroque scenes that art critics didn't appreciate.

Meanwhile, in one of the tenement buildings a local boy on the other end of the economic spectrum, Ralph Fasanella, began in the 1940s to paint scenes from the Italian section of Greenwich Village as well as studies of working people and subject matter suggestive of his Communist inclinations. Fasanella, who has been compared to Grandma Moses, worked in a primitive and at times surrealist style. One painting shows his father, an iceman, on a cross with ice tongs as his crown of thorns. Another is a detailed scene of a May Day parade and yet another protests the execution of the Rosenbergs. Like Stella, Fasanella did a painting of *Coney Island*, but his canvas shows working people enjoying the beach as a break from their every day world.

Ralph lived in the same tenement as my mother and she remembered his whole family. She remembered their identical apartments on different floors and the gas meter into which she slipped quarters to get heat. She recalled how she and other neighborhood children would pick up coal that had fallen from delivery trucks and wondered why the trucks didn't stop very often at their buildings. She didn't know what I later learned: the coal trucks were afraid to stop in that neighborhood, because the poverty of the area had given it a bad reputation. Yet my mother felt perfectly safe there. The young men of the area were known to watch out for the young girls to make sure that no strangers bothered them.

Years later I met Fasanella when he visited Rhode Island, where I was living at that time, to talk about his art. The newspaper article announcing his talk mentioned that he was brought up in the building next door to one where Mayor LaGuardia had lived. Since I knew my mother's original apartment was located next door to LaGuardia's birthplace on Thompson Street, I introduced myself to Fasanella, who was thrilled to meet someone from the "old neighborhood," as he said.

He was a school dropout who spoke bitterly to me about

being sent to reform school because he played hooky so often. Being taken away from his family and placed in an institution had been traumatic.

An autodidact, he was passionate in his dedication to the rights of workers. As a young man he had worked as a union organizer. Not only did his paintings, teeming with detail, express his political point of view, but he also talked nonstop with frequent references to his readings about his working-class commitment. He was a lively and engaging conversationalist and it was not unusual for the two of us when we met at various conferences to talk well into the night. A passionate partisan, he attributed his political thought to his mother (a button hole maker), who, he told me, had urged him to fight in the Spanish Civil War. He had joined the Abraham Lincoln Brigade, many of whose members were Communist sympathizers.

To support his family while he painted, he pumped gas in his brother's garage and his wife taught school. Toward the end of his life, he had a different perspective on the hardships he had undergone for his art. He thought it had been good for him to struggle because out of that struggle a toughness and perspective had emerged. When he told me this, I suspected that he felt that his son, who went on to become a graphic artist, had neither the passion nor the toughness that Ralph possessed. He feared for his son but perhaps he failed to realize that his son—who was named after Vito Marcantonio, the Socialist Congressman from Italian Harlem and a protégé of Fiorello La Guardia—

didn't need that kind of toughness.

My father was a great admirer of the Little Flower who had worked so hard for immigrants, first at Ellis Island and then as mayor. According to Thomas Kestner's biography, La Guardia was responsible for making New York a modern city with his early proposal to build an airport, among other initiatives. He was also influential on a national level and proposed several New Deal programs to President Franklin Roosevelt. But for us kids, he was the man who read us the funnies over the radio every Sunday.

Another immigrant who toiled in the arts from that neighborhood, for the most part in obscurity, was Joseph Cautela. He was a barber who wrote book reviews and a novel, *Moon Harvest,* about an Italian immigrant couple. The husband has an affair with an American woman who introduces him to the artistic life of the city. Torn between this soulful connection and his lifeless marriage, in the end he turns his back on art, does his duty, and stays with his wife. By chance, I met the author's grandson Tony (whose wife worked in the same law office as my husband) who was doing corporate writing, but harbored not very secret yearnings to do more creative work. He confirmed that his grandfather had been rumored to have affairs and that the liaison in the book may have been based on fact.

But if the arts were in the immigrant air, they were no more so than in Washington Square Park. Every spring the park was the site of an art exhibit, started by Willem

DeKooning and Jackson Pollack in the early 1930s. Artists hung their work with wires on the fence surrounding the park and the displays often spread up Fifth Avenue or down onto the Judson Church's property. The artists would sit amidst their paintings hoping to sell a few. Sometimes they'd sit at an easel and continue with their work. They were always ready to chat with the public, even those like us kids who weren't in the market for buying. I enjoyed talking to them. For me, they represented 'real' Americans, that is, those who had been here longer than we.

One year Judson Church opted out of the exhibit. I don't know if they disapproved of some of the art or if there were other reasons for this. This was well before the imitations of the Margaret Keane's girls with large sad eyes that proliferated in the sixties, which even I, whose tastes were probably shaped partly by the art I saw at the earlier exhibitions, recognized as marking the end of authentic art coming out of the Village.

As I remember, the paintings were often still lifes, portraits, landscapes, and what we generally called "modern art." There was nothing very objectionable, though there was always a scattering of nudes. My mother bought one of these, an imitation of *September Morn,* depicting a nude woman up to her calves in the sea and holding a towel strategically placed below her navel and flowing to her knees. My mother also bought a still life of flowers that I've always loved, done in the manner of the old masters. Another, a large oil of a wind-tossed ship, she hung on the wall over our piano.

My own memories of Judson Church are connected with Judson House, located behind the church at Thompson and 3rd Streets. Hardly an architectural gem, Judson House—a dirty gray fortress-like building, long since torn down—held children's programs, which I attended. One was a cooking class, a photo of which finds me sifting flour with a fellow student in the basement of the building. My nose with its white smudge shows traces of my handiwork. My brother Tom remembers taking cooking classes there as well, where he learned how to prepare breakfast foods such as scrambled eggs and the never popular oatmeal. When I asked him if they then sat down and ate what they prepared, he answered, "Unfortunately, yes."

My brother's favorite "breakfast" which he ate at night before going to bed was a large bowl of Italian bread and milk. It had been a favorite of my mother's and it was, of course, she who introduced him to this thoroughly uninteresting dish from my perspective. But oatmeal was never on either of our lists of breakfasts; as for eggs, we usually ate them on weekends.

As a matter of fact, like a lot of Italians we were not big on breakfast during the week, probably because we were always in a hurry to get to school on time. My mother finally concocted an "egg-shake" for me by mixing milk, Ovaltine, and a raw egg in a mixer she had bought to make malteds.

The cooking classes were part of an effort to wean Italian immigrants away from their cuisine, considered unhealthy because of its low consumption of meat and lots of, what food reformers of the time called, "watery" vegetables, such as *scarole*, dandelions and other greens. The Italians prized such foods because they believed these greens cleared the system naturally.

Generally failing to change the cooking habits of the adults—few Italian immigrants liked the bland recipes they presented—the reformers reasoned that they could achieve their goals by targeting the children and teaching them nutritional cooking á la reformers' formulas. I doubt that many of these children, when they became adults, replaced their tasty Italian food with the 'foreign' recipes of the food reformers. And yet my mother, who lacked the "benefit" of American cooking classes, made us mashed potatoes every night and my brother and I ordered a turkey dinner with those same potatoes when we dined out with our parents on Sundays.

Another class that I remember taking at Judson House was art. All these years later I can distinctly recall one painting I did of an angel because I was so disappointed in it. The angel has yellow hair, my perception of the angelic, and wears a pink gown, but that's not the problem. What's wrong with the angel's body is that it's totally graceless, straight up and down with no lovely little waist or curved pose. Instead she's squat and fat, looking straight at the viewer—most unlike the angels of popular iconography.

Another institution I attended was Greenwich House, founded in 1902 and located off Greenwich Avenue in a nondescript brick building on Barrow Street. It had a large auditorium with a stage, where dramatics classes were held as well as many smaller rooms used for dance and other studies. It emphasized the arts. It had been founded as a settlement house for immigrants, but by the time I attended in the late nineteen forties it had become known throughout New York City for its drama classes. I remember my first class assignment at age ten or eleven when we had to prepare a dramatic reading of a children's story. I chose something that had to do with mice and I changed my voice for each character. The teacher praised my rendition and I was pleased with my 'performance.' But this self-satisfaction proved to be short-lived when auditions for a major play occurred. One of the young girls, who had traveled all the way from the Bronx, gave an outstanding reading by adding gestures at her audition. I still remember how, in her character's prim demeanor, she mimed touching a table to see if it was dusty: a finger dragged along a table, a quick look at the finger, nose in the air and then a flourish of the hand in dismissal.

My best friend lived on West 10th Street between Fifth and Sixth Avenues, opposite the English Terrace row houses. Sheila and I saw the houses every time we stepped out her front door. Started in 1856, these homes were the first to be built without the high Dutch stoops that lined the residences of Washington Square Park North.

Even earlier, in 1829, Aaron Burr had Federal row houses built for himself on MacDougal Street between 3rd and 4th Streets, next door to what became the Provincetown Playhouse at number 133. Edna St. Vincent Millay first performed there in one of her own plays and it's where I saw *The Fantasticks*. The theater was small and intimate—a perfect venue for such a show in that the high energy level of the singing and dancing jumped right out at the audience, seeming to pull us right into the action. Its love story was poignant with loss and longing and the lyrics to the songs were poetic. "Who understands," one song asked, "why we all must die a bit/before we grow again?" The experience was much like the one I had at my first Broadway show, *Peter Pan*, when I clapped for Tinker-Bell until my hands hurt.

My best friend's father was a dentist who had his office on the ground floor of their brownstone. It seems that dentists took over many of the lovely nineteenth-century buildings. My own dentist had his office on Washington Place near where Henry James was born in 1843. James feared the immigrants' "conquest of New York," but that conquest occurred in a way he hadn't expected. They became educated and acculturated.

James's maternal grandparents lived at 19 Washington Square North, next door to my grammar school, St. Joseph Academy, at number 20. Their house began a block-long stretch of lovely Greek Revival structures that survive to this day. On the other side of my school was a narrow four-story building that, as far as I was concerned, was known for housing two great Danes. They were the attraction, standing proud and lean. No one sitting in the park opposite could take their eyes off the dogs—whether from fear, astonishment or admiration, I'll never know—as they emerged from the front door at the top of the long Dutch-style stoop.

Back on Fifth Avenue at 11ʰ Street stands the First Presbyterian Church of New York, the same one that had ministered to the Italian immigrants in the building bought by the Little Red School House. The turrets of the church reminded me of the sand-dripped towers we built at the beach. The church was modeled after St. Savior Church in Bath, England and its tower resembled that of Magdalen College at Oxford.

It is a much fussier edifice than the Episcopal Church of the Ascension one block downtown at 10th Street with its tower modeled on another one in Oxford. The Episcopal Church now has National Historic Landmark status. Willa Cather, the writer who lived in the Village at one time, was particularly fond of John LaFarge's great fresco above the altar of the Church of the Ascension. In 1904 another LaFarge, C. Grant LaFarge, was responsible for a very different kind of art, found under the city's streets.

He designed some of the most interesting New York City subway art, as Lee Stookey tells us in her book on the subject. At Astor Place in the Village on the IRT line, we have one of the most beautiful station signs. At the top is a decorative terra cotta cornice with vases and scrolls. Below is the name tablet with its distinctive colors and lettering. At each side of the name tablet is the image of a beaver, chosen to represent the basis of the fortune that John Jacob Astor amassed in the fur trade. Equally beautiful, but very different, are the design and lettering used at the Bleecker Street station, another gem, on the IRT line. Besides the faience surrounding the name tablet with its distinctive lettering is a large capital B entwined by tulips and referring to an early Dutch landowner whose name marks the street.

Squire Vickers followed LaFarge as a subway designer in 1916, but in a very different style. "Arts and Crafts restraint gave way to the Machine Age," according to *The New York Times* of August 2, 2007. Gone are the curves and scrolls of the earlier designs, replaced by geometric abstractions, handsome in their own "clean" way. One that I saw every weekday for four years was the name tablet at 86th Street, where I exited the Lexington Avenue line to attend my high school.

At the turn of the century Willa Cather lived on Washington Square South. It was here that she wrote her Nebraska novels about an earlier generation of immigrants from Germany, Sweden, Bohemia, Czechoslovakia, Norway and French Canada. In *O! Pioneers*, Carl Linstrom says of his move to the big city that "we have no house, no place, no people of our own. We live in the streets, in the parks, in the theatres. We sit in restaurants and concert halls and look about at the hundreds of our own kind and shudder."

The Italian immigrants who settled in Greenwich Village did not share Linstrom's attitude. They took to the city and made the Village their neighborhood because, despite being farmers, they were urbanites at heart. They had lived in what historians call "agrotowns," a poor choice of words perhaps, in that it suggests a recently put-up town to accommodate workers. But these towns had been there for centuries, perhaps even millennia. Unlike the French peasants who worked the land around their houses, Italian farming villages had their houses clustered together with the land they farmed a long distance away. The peasants "commuted" to their lands in the valleys for as much as two hours in each direction. And "commuting" for them meant walking. Often they had to commute again after reaching their land because of the inheritance system whereby each sibling inherited some good land in one location and some poor land in another, necessitating travel between both parcels.

Generally speaking, Italian immigrants shunned farming in America. They had had enough of its disappointments in Italy with crop failures and repaying high interest loans. Besides, they could make in nine months of construction work what would have taken them a year to earn by farming—without running the risk of crop failure. A workman in America spent 41% of his salary on food while it Italy he had had to spend almost

85%. No wonder the immigrants went after construction and factory work. At the turn of the century, they were willing to dig subway tunnels with all the dangers involved in such work, rather than farm.

A few Italian immigrants participated in attempts to relocate from the cities. Two settlements in Alabama, in Daphne and Lambert, were modestly successful. Two other such settlements were founded in Arkansas as well, one in Sunnyside, which was plagued by malaria and the other in Tontitown in the Ozarks. Nativists in the area twice burned down Tontitown. Other rural settlements suffered from the usual difficulties connected with farming and the immigrants continued to favor cities.

Next door to Willa Cather's house, at 61 Washington Square South, also known as 4th Street, was the "House of Genius," called that because so many writers, such as Frank Norris, lived there. (The confusing nomenclature of the Village was further confounded by its warren of twisting streets. At one point 4th Street and 10th Street, planned as parallel blocks everywhere else, intersect each other.) Down the block during the same era lived Lincoln Steffens, the journalist and muckraker, and John Reed, a journalist, Communist, and staff member of *The Masses*, a radical magazine. His book, *Ten Days that Shook the World*, gives a detailed account of the November 1917 Russian Revolution.

Reed was arrested in 1913 for speaking on behalf of the striking silk workers in Paterson, New Jersey. He went on to write a "Pageant of the Paterson Strike." Pageants were popular entertainments of the time and this one was performed in Madison Square Garden to raise money for the workers, many of whom were Italian. Carlo Tresca was one of the leaders of the strike, and another Italian who played an important role was Pietro Botto. He came from Northern Italy, home to so many silk workers in an industry that was widespread there. I remember reading about Rosa Cassettari who at age six was learning the trade by scalding her fingers in boiling water.

Botto arrived in America in 1892 and by 1907 he had saved enough money to buy land and build a house in nearby Haledon, New Jersey. Italians were notorious for their zealous saving, living in want today for a better future tomorrow. The fifteen years Botto took to buy his land and build his house seem to support this. His wife cooked for boarders in two three-room apartments they rented out on their second floor. She also worked at home as a "picker," a skilled job of examining the finished silk fabric for flaws. She and her husband—though a weaver, he was not a member of the IWW—allowed the leaders of the strike, Elizabeth Gurley Flynn and Big Bill Haywood along with Tresca, to rally the strikers from their second floor balcony, thus imparting the unity and cohesiveness needed to maintain the strike.

But those days of intense labor agitation were long over when I was a child. When I was growing up, the big issue involved the housing squeeze. NYU wanted to build its law library. All the Italian Americans living south of the park were opposed to this expansion from the original building at Washington Place on the west side of the park. But NYU prevailed and eventually took over the site of my first grammar school on Washington Square South, building a formidable rose-colored edifice that had intimations of an Egyptian temple with its broad expanses of solid stone, thick as a fortress. Nowadays excluding its medical and dental schools, NYU owns about sixty buildings with 9.3 million square feet. The community that now fights further expansion has few Italian Americans left, owing to the exodus of the college-educated second generation in the nineteen sixties. The current inhabitants, who gentrified the neighborhood, recently protested NYU's planned law school expansion on West Third Street, where the university wants to replace a town house where Edgar Allan Poe once lived as well as a set of row houses renovated by McKim, Mead and White. Once again NYU prevailed.

The Grosvenor Hotel with its mirrors and graceful columns in the lobby decorated with gold leaves is still on Fifth Avenue, but it was long ago taken over by New York University. When my daughter attended the university in 1982, she lived in the hotel and enjoyed its lovely lobby. More changes, I'm sure, will come to the Village and NYU will be responsible for many of them.

Of less architectural interest, but noteworthy nonetheless, is Parrazzo's Funeral Home (now called the

Greenwich Village Funeral Home) diagonally across from the Little Red School House on Bleecker Street. It has a beautiful curved stained glass window over its entryway. Inside is an historic photo of the neighborhood that has come out to mourn the first of its sons, the first Italian-American soldier, killed in World War I. As the funeral cortege drives by, the streets are carpeted with people. They spill over into the street. They cover the fire escapes. They hang from lampposts. This is a whole neighborhood that has come to mourn one of its own. I can only imagine the loss that this immigrant family felt with the death of their son and the death of their hopes for a new life in the new world.

My mother's brother, my Uncle Louie, was also in World War I for about six months—on the side of Italy. He had been unable to enter America in 1907 with the rest of the family because of an eye disease, probably trachoma, and had to return to Italy. During his time there, he trained as both a tailor and a barber. Finally at age sixteen he was allowed entry into New York and a year or two after that he was drafted into the Italian army and had to return to Italy to serve. Or at least that's what my mother told me.

But when I was checking my facts by calling my uncle's son, Lou, he told me that his father chose the American Army on October 25, 1918 and was discharged by December 5th, 1918. He became an American citizen in 1919. In that war Italian immigrants, if they weren't yet citizens, could make a choice as to which army to serve in, since the U.S. and Italy were allies. Did my mother's version of the story suggest that she felt greater loyalty to Italy than to America and so she remembered her brother's service in the way she did? Is that another possible explanation for her delaying her own citizenship until 1927? Or like me, did she appreciate more the drama of the story that he had served in the Italian Army? My preference for his having served in the Italian Army emphasized the dual loyalty and identification immigrants felt towards their country of birth and their adopted one.

When my father received a summons to serve in the U.S. Army during World War I, he promptly tore up the notice. He had received it on November 11, 1918. I don't know if he opened his mailbox on the eleventh hour, when the Armistice occurred, of that eleventh day of the eleventh month that we still celebrate as Veterans' Day, but I do know that no repercussions followed his tearing up of his draft notice. The U. S. government was a looser entity then. And besides, the war was over, soldiers would soon be mustered out of the armed services and the draft ended.

By the time of the Second World War, Italian Americans viewed fighting in the war for America as an opportunity to demonstrate their patriotism. Some felt tainted by the support some prominent Italian Americans gave to Mussolini early on and wanted to dispel any notions of their not being loyal Americans. Parents took the death of their sons stoically though they must have felt the same grief as the parents of that first World War I son to die from the Italian neighborhood of the Village.

One early supporter of Mussolini was Generoso Pope, who published the newspaper, *Il Progresso Italo-Americano*. When America declared war on Italy, Pope abandoned his support of Mussolini. He went on to found the *National Enquirer*, a tabloid of dubious distinction. Other ordinary Italian Americans also supported Mussolini and his dreams of empire, many because they viewed his ambitions and dreams of glory as a compensation for the discrimination they felt in their new land.

Common among the streets of the Italian section of Greenwich Village were 'social' clubs. Initially started as mutual aid societies of people from the same Italian town, by the 1940s with less need of such security, many had evolved into clubs for men to play cards and drink espresso in a generally smoky atmosphere. But one club was different: the Progressive Era Club on Waverly Place. Prominent Italians, such as George Bragalini, a banker with Manufacturers Hanover Trust Company who became the New York State Commissioner of Taxation and Finance and later Acting Postmaster, were members. Bragalini had been one of the first Italian Americans to graduate from Stuyvesant High School, an elite public school in Manhattan.

The Progressive Era Club seemed to be a political club, which was a holdover from the early days of the century when the Progressive Party concerned itself with issues of immigration and child welfare laws. Though hardly prominent, my father was a member and attended various evening meetings held there as well as dinners the club sponsored. His interest in such issues doesn't surprise me given his own impoverished beginnings as an immigrant.

Culinary and Other Matters

Not only was the Village of my day filled with noteworthy high culture in the form of architecture but it also had wonderful ordinary culture in the form of food stores: I'd accompany my grandmother to a number of vegetable stores where she would bargain for the freshest greens with the owners. The produce stores on Thompson Street were often dark rooms with worn wooden floors. What light there was came through the door, always open. A large central area remained empty for customers to select their produce, bargain with the owner, often in shadow and seated on a stool, its back incomplete and broken, and gossip with the other customers. Crates, pushed against the walls, housed the *scarole*, Swiss chard and other vegetables in the same packing that the wholesaler provider. The owners didn't stress presentation. This was in contrast with the produce on Bleecker Street, west of Sixth. Those fruit and vegetable stores opposite Pompeii Church were subtle hymns to the incarnate: owners displayed oranges next to red peppers, red peppers near pale green fennel, pale fennel next to dark spinach, spinach near yellow bananas, bananas next to burgundy beets. A square of cardboard held up by a little stick pushed into the middle of the produce crate displaying the price, the writing often with a European flair to its script.

To me the "rollers," used to move crates of food into the stores, were almost as eye-catching as the colorful food displays. The cellar "elevators" were truly 'lifts' that rose up from the ground beneath two flat metal doors splayed open to ease the movement of food boxes from both above and below.

On Sullivan Street alone, down from Houston, was Bruno's Bakery with its fresh bread aroma swirling out its door; *Gourmet* magazine eventually 'discovered' Joe's cheese store next door with its freshly made ricotta and mozzarella along with cacciocavallo and—my favorite— basket cheese, a farmer's cheese that took on the basket's pattern. I liked the brown woven basket as much as the cheese itself. Next to it was a no-name candy store that sold Charlotte Russe, a spongy cake topped with whipped cream; further down was another no-name candy store with penny candy—that really cost only a penny. It wasn't actually a store large enough to enter. It simply had the penny candy displayed on a slanted board facing the street with the owner standing behind it. I'd take what I wanted from the display and pass the pennies over the counter for the little colored dots of sugar on white strips of paper, among others. This 'store' was right next to the

Chinese laundry, where I'd see the Chinese man sweating over an iron when my mother brought in my father's shirts to be done with 'a little starch.' My mother knew that if she said 'a little starch,' a little starch is what she'd get. She couldn't count on the regular laundry to do my father's shirts the way he liked them. We never conversed with the Chinese laundry man as we did with the other vendors because we couldn't speak each other's language so that he and the other workers always remained a people of mystery.

During certain times of the year, a small cart with clams on the half shell appeared around the corner on Prince and Thompson Streets. The shallow cart was filled with crushed ice. Workmen would gather around it to eat their fill of clams, the owner shucking the clams as quickly as another person might crack open a nut. Occasionally my mother approached the stand when no workmen were about. I think she considered it embarrassing in some way when the men surrounded the stand to put herself forward in that way. When she was pregnant with me, my father hollered at her for not buying the clams when she had, as they said in the dialect, a 'wuogli' (pronounced 'woolie,' accent on the second syllable), a desire for them. I think the word was a corruption of 'vuole,' 'you want' or 'desire', in standard Italian. In any case pregnant women were supposed to satisfy their cravings for the good of their future child.

On that same corner was a grocery store owned by a Jewish man, whom my mother rarely patronized. She felt loyalty to the Italian store-owners of the neighborhood. Koreans, who now dominate New York City's grocery trade with their flowers displayed on the sidewalk in front of their stores along with fruits and vegetables, now operate that grocery store.

Owners of such stores put in eighteen-hour days. Their whole family helps to make the business successful. First the father must get up in the middle of the night and drive a long distance to get the best produce at the wholesaler's market. Once he returns, the whole family must pick over the greens, tearing away any unsightly leaves, polishing the apples and arranging the produce in neat rows. Then they must take turns manning the store for many long hours. Such a procedure reminds me of the stories I heard from my parents about the hard work performed and the long hours that the Italian immigrants put in. If the Chinese are the Italian of the East, the Koreans are the new Italians of New York City.

The hardware store across the street from the apartment building where I grew up is now a Korean-owned grocery store too. High-end stores and art galleries, like Dolce and Gabbana and the Franklin Bowles Gallery, dot the first floor of buildings on the street. Next door to where I grew up is a building that was painted a dull battleship gray when I lived there. Now it's a beautiful bright white building, showing off its stately columns that used to fade into the gray background.

Back on Sullivan Street opposite Bruno's bakery was Virginia's delicatessen, all a bustle on Sunday mornings, everyone milling about in front of the counter, behind which stood Virginia, the proprietor, always smiling her owlish smile despite the hubbub of relentless activity compressed into a few short hours. Barrels of olives lined the way to the counter. Wheels of cheese to be sliced and delicatessen meats to be devoured gave off pungent odors that made stomachs' growl, particularly those who had fasted since midnight in order to receive Holy Communion. A fan hung from the tin ceiling, impressed with geometric designs. A natural businesswoman, known for her shrewd business sense, Virginia, her eyes sparkling behind her gold-rimmed glasses, always gave out extra thin slices of salami or proscuitto or whatever a mother was buying to the child accompanying her.

Next door to Virginia's was St. Anthony of Padua Church (its façade seen in *The Godfather* during the baptism and murder mayhem scene), an imposing gray stone structure with a rose window, where on Good Friday the elderly women, my grandmother included, would process around the church and sing the most plangent hymns I ever heard. All the sorrows of their lives poured into those religious melodies.

My mother and her sister were not particularly religious women. We had no crucifixes hanging on our walls or pictures of saints under glass. We did have one statue standing on my mother's dresser of Christ the King because my parents were married on his feast day in October. The size of a small doll, the statue had a young boy's face and wore a crown. Its regal look, rendered by its painted royal robes so dominated the statue that I found it difficult to think of it as Jesus, whom we always saw depicted wearing a tunic and sandals. I was never quite sure what to make of that statue with its worldly connotations.

Although my mother made sure my brother and I attended Mass every Sunday, she was too busy to attend when we were small. Instead she'd send us with my grandmother or my godmother. When we attended with my grandmother, we would go to the 'Italian' Mass, in which the pastor, known for his kindness and gentility, delivered the sermon in Italian. He was eventually replaced by his exact opposite, Father A. Whereas the old priest had shiny black hair, wore gold-rimmed glasses, and tended towards being plump, the new pastor was lean and angular with a broken nose. The dominant impression of him was of someone ready for a fight. He thundered from the pulpit not only about our sins but also the sins of prominent Italians, such as baseball great Joe DiMaggio when he married actress Marilyn Monroe.

Father A. was not popular in my family, nor was he loved as the old pastor had been. This priest was a working class kid who talked tough and had finally 'made it' to pastor whereas the old pastor was a well-educated, caring

Italian priest. The first thing the new pastor did was to embark on a money-raising campaign to repair the church and the sisters' quarters. While no doubt needed, stories were told about his shaming and bullying poor people to donate beyond their means.

I'm sure he had good qualities as well, but I never heard of them at home. He tried to rid the Village of its drug dealers, men I didn't know existed in our neighborhood. Father A. wanted his parishioners to inform him about which of the young men were dealing drugs. He thought he could break the code of silence that dominated the Italian neighborhood, but he was unable to. The very characteristic which allowed the Italians to live amicably with their diverse neighbors was the characteristic which would not allow them to interfere with another's person's life: they were aware that conditions in life sometimes led people to make unwise decisions and they were not going to interfere with that right. In other words, they extended, rightly or not, their live-and-let-live attitude to drug dealers.

Further along on Bleecker Street across Sixth Avenue was the only pork store the Italian neighborhood women trusted enough to buy their sausages in the belief that they were stuffed with nothing but good clean meat. This was at a time when my father still recalled Upton Sinclair's expose of the meat packing industry with rats and other unsavory ingredients in hot dogs and sausages.

A few blocks away on Prince Street was Vesuvio's

bakery, owned by Mr. Zito, his hair as black and shiny as an olive. I marveled at the pattern the many air holes in his crunchy hardtack bread, my personal favorite, made. Around another corner on Houston Street was Raffetto's pasta store where we bought our pasta for homemade ravioli on the holidays. After church my grandmother would start to mix the ricotta, eggs, grated cheese and parsley together for the filling. She then added salt and pepper to taste. I would watch her closely, waiting until she'd ask me my opinion of the creamy mixture.

"Does it need more salt, Carol, or pepper?"

I'd scoop out a heaping teaspoon of the filling and savor it. It was always perfect.

Then she'd begin to put a spoonful down on the large sheet of pasta, eyeing the distance between that spoonful and the next and checking it with the width of her finger. Once one row was finished, she'd fold the dough over the filling, take her cutting wheel and mark the pasta into little squares. Out would come her fork with its tines to press the edges of each small fluffy pillow of pasta to keep the luscious filling from escaping. Then she'd start on the next row until all the pasta was used. If I was lucky, I'd get any left over filling to savor, scraping the bowl beyond decency. Once the ravioli were assembled, she'd place dishtowels on the twin beds in the back bedroom, spread out the ravioli and cover them with more dishtowels until it was time to cook them. All over the Village other grandmothers and mothers used the same method of storing ravioli until cooking time.

Our holiday menus never varied. We'd start with an antipasto of the thinnest possible slices of Genoa salami— thin slices was the only way to savor it—along with roasted red peppers dripping in oil, anchovies, and olives, black and green. The black ones were the wrinkled Sicilian kind; the green were stuffed with red pimento. I was in charge of arranging this platter decoratively, taking the time to lay down the salami slices in overlapping rounds creating a scallop pattern, heaping the red peppers in a mound in the center of the plate, placing the olives just so, and sprinkling the anchovies about. Our homemade ravioli followed this first course. Next came the roast: turkey for Thanksgiving, roast beef at Christmas, and leg of lamb at Easter. Then along with stuffed artichokes, a mixed salad and pastries, which early in the morning my father would buy at Ferraro's Bakery on Grand Street on the Lower East Side. And for us kids, torrone, the sugar and egg-white confection dotted with almonds and covered with a thin wafer, which, though I knew it wasn't, I treated like communion because of its being a replica of that sacrament. And finally a beautiful tray of fresh fruits topped by grapes, and with dried figs, dates and nuts.

Often at our holiday meals, my mother invited her oldest friend, Viola, from her grammar school days. A blowsy, middle-aged single woman who wore too much make-up, Viola had a throaty laugh and a smoky voice. Her blouses always seemed to spill over her skirt, yet strain at her bosom, and her shoes were too big for her feet while at the same time the top of her feet seemed stuffed into too small an area. Her hair was patchy and dull. Yet for all this she was the beloved mistress of a married Jewish lawyer, named Harold.

Viola had had a hard life. She had suffered from a nervous breakdown. Though I never understood what this meant, I pictured some amorphous kind of physical break. But what I understood by it was that that was the reason she could never hold a job. She needed a job where she could first of all sleep late, and one that wouldn't tax her in any way. And she needed to be the one to define its parameters.

She hadn't finished college so that closed off the usual women's occupations of the time of teacher, librarian or nurse—if she could have found such positions that started at mid-morning, one of her prerequisites. Viola belonged to that generation of women who were very capable, but not allowed, for the most part, to express themselves in any but the traditional female occupations. Her intelligence and flamboyance fascinated me. An extremely bright woman, who spoke articulately on a range of subjects, she would have made a good professor or a lawyer instead of falling in love with one.

She was also trapped by her relationship with Harold. The laws in New York State were such that Harold couldn't get a divorce unless he admitted to adultery. He was not about to do that and risk losing most of his assets. So he and Viola went along as they did for more than twenty years at that point. When the divorce laws in New York finally liberalized, Harold still remained married. His wife was sickly, he said, and he couldn't leave her. I didn't believe this for a moment and felt that he liked things just as they were; yet I sympathized with Harold. I understood that living with Viola day in and day out would have been a trial for anyone. And I think Harold knew this too.

Perhaps on some level Viola understood her situation too. She danced a delicate balance between asking him for money and working odd jobs to support herself. But she was dependent on him economically. My mother also came to her financial aid from time to time.

Despite her blowsy manner and lipstick that ran into the crevices of her lips like so many exclamation points, Viola was a witty woman with a great sense of humor and an infectious laugh. She was also a chain smoker: smoke would burst from her nostrils when she laughed, making more emphatic her seemingly indomitable spirit. I liked her a lot.

But she must have remained vulnerable at heart. A measure of her desperation perhaps, was that, at one point, she put my mother down as a reference for taking care of two young children. Even then at my age of about thirteen or so, I couldn't imagine Viola caring for young children. Though she enjoyed my brother and me, she didn't seem very maternal. Her considering such a position told me how desperate she was for both money and some regularity in her life. When she died many years later, my mother told me that at the funeral Harold blubbered like a baby.

At these holiday dinners my grandmother didn't prepare the fancy pastries, the *sfogliatelle, babas au rhum* and *cannoli* that we bought at Ferrara's on Grand Street on the Lower East Side or that you could eat on MacDougal Street along with a cup of cappuccino at Caffe Reggio with its decoratively carved benches of dark wood. But she did bake on the holidays: at Christmas it was *struffoli,* little fried balls of eggy dough, dipped in honey and candy sprinkles—very festive. On St. Joseph's feast day of March 19th, she'd fried *zeppoli,* large donuts covered with confectioner's sugar. They were mouth-watering when eaten hot out of the pot. At Easter, she baked the round Easter breads, imbedded with hard-boiled eggs, their shells covered with sprinkles and held in place with a strip of dough.

My grandmother baked all these things without recipes—her memory was impressive, filled as well with long funny stories in rhyme. These rhyming stories often concerned mishaps and minor tragedies that were told in a comedic vein, diffusing the misery of the situation. Comedy transformed troublesome events into fodder for a good story to amuse others and to prevent a person from taking herself or himself too seriously. Characters' foibles were exposed and egos were deflated. When I was in high school, a Jesuit retreat master taught a similar lesson by calling to mind the words of a popular song: "Life is just a bowl of cherries/Don't take it serious/It's too mysterious" as he emphasized the great mystery and unknowableness of God.

As for my grandmother's baking skills, she knew the batter was right by the feel and look of the thing. Consequently we have very few recipes that were handed down through the family.

In obtaining the recipe for my godmother's meatballs—every Italian family has one member's meatballs singled out as the outstanding ones; it's part of the folklore—it reads to this day as two handfuls of breadcrumbs, four or five eggs depending. Depending on what is not specified. It depends on the maker's feel for the mix on that day, whether it is a high moisture day or a low humidity one—or whatever.

Starting at about age six, my mother gave me wine mixed with water at dinnertime. I really didn't like the taste of the wine that much. What I liked was the little burgundy colored glass in which it was served. The glass was thick with triangular cuts projecting out from it—I liked feeling the little patterns that formed—and shaped like an elongated goblet.

Though great Italian food shops existed in the Village, in those days, not a great number of good restaurants existed. Those there were mainly of the spaghetti and meatball type, which we could do ourselves at home, only better. So when at a certain point we started going out to dinner every Sunday to give my mother a break from cooking, we drove up to Schmidt's Farm Restaurant in Westchester. We drove up the West Side Highway along the Hudson River, always beautiful and with its own special lighting, and through some then rural sections of Westchester, my mother pointing out cows in fields along the way.

Driving there also had the benefit of satisfying an activity that Americans of that era engaged in, namely taking a drive just for the sake of taking a drive. It was the era of the American romance with the car, a romance that had been suppressed during the war years, due to gasoline rationing, and cars that were nursed to survive since the automotive industry was on hold while planes and tanks were produced.

The restaurant served American cooking, the secrets of which eluded my mother. Though she always tried her best at American cooking, she didn't have a feel for it. Mashed potatoes were lumpy; she started chicken á la king using a can of Campbell mushroom soup.

But Schmidt's Farm was the real American food thing as far as we all were concerned. For $2.75 I ate a meal starting with shrimp cocktail—I was always an adventurous eater—homemade cream of chicken soup, a turkey entrée with stuffing, gravy, silky mashed potatoes and a vegetable, and a dessert which surprisingly I no longer remember: in our house, we were not big on dessert; fruit was usually served. My brother and I could never finish our turkey entrée, so my mother would take a roll and fix a sandwich with our leftover turkey for my brother and me to eat on our drive home. Before the journey home, we'd all take a brisk walk around the extensive grounds of the restaurant.

Often neighbors of ours, Jack and Frances, a couple with grown children, whom my parents had helped to get the highly desirable apartment above ours, accompanied us to Schmidt's Farm. Each of my parents liked the family very much. My father and Jack were best friends, yet each was so very different from the other, it was hard to understand the basis of the friendship. Jack was tall and slim and my father was short and round. By the standards of my neighborhood, Jack was an educated man and my father was not. Jack was well spoken and my father, rough spoken; Jack was pious, my father anticlerical. Jack had a salesman's way about him: affable with a ready laugh and always some flattering comments to make. My father never flattered anyone, but he did have a ready laugh. I think this was part of the basis of their friendship as well as the fact that, though Jack had had more schooling than my father, he respected my father's native intelligence as well as his directness and honesty.

My mother appreciated Jack because he was tall and slim and spoke a Piemontese dialect that was closer to standard Italian than her Calabrian one. This gentleman also had a charm about him and genteel manners that my mother yearned for. Like many women of her generation, she as a secretary was introduced to middle-class America while the men often remained in their working-class world. As a secretary in the office of Reo Cars, a manufacturer located 'uptown' and outside the neighborhood, my mother saw a class of people she admired and she assimilated into American ways quickly.

But her interactions with Jack made her put on airs occasionally in both English and Italian. Jack would speak in both languages in deference to my grandmother who only spoke Italian. A three-way conversation between my mother, grandmother and Jack would ensue. My mother thought of Jack as educated and was awed by the way he spoke standard Italian. Her attempts to make rejoinders in the standard Italian she had picked up over the years were almost always successful. I enjoyed listening to them both and could hear the beauty of the Italian language as they spoke.

My mother was a quick study who never gave herself credit for speaking standard Italian well. She had no confidence in her abilities and wouldn't attend certain functions where women who spoke the standard language would be in attendance for fear of shaming herself with her version of the language. I was confused by her reluctance to speak the standard Italian with the women because she so obviously took great delight and satisfaction in speaking it to Jack, who loved my mother's adulation. He seemed to stand even taller than his six-foot height as my mother signaled her approbation with smiles and lustrous eyes. But perhaps that dynamic would have been missing in her interactions with the women, with whom she would have felt in competition. I've always wondered what her hesitation was really about.

Jack had a difficult work situation in that he worked as a manager for a relative in a large bakery, known for its breadsticks, which serviced many restaurants in New York. Because he was well-spoken and knew how to flatter restaurateurs, Jack was the person who called upon these restaurants for their orders. He had been promised that when the relative who owned the bakery died he would inherit the business. But nothing was in writing. It was a terrible predicament to be in. His desire to be the owner spurred him on to work long hours growing the business. Ultimately the business was not left to him and he felt betrayed.

My father enjoyed Frances who as a young woman had been a dancer—even as a plump forty-something-year-old (which I thought of as old) she was limber and able to entertain us by doing a split—and who had a great sense of humor and a verve about her that my mother lacked. Jack enjoyed my mother's adoration and Frances appreciated my father joining her in fun and laughter. Moreover my parents both liked being appreciated for qualities that their own spouses no longer were impressed by. Even as a pre-teen, I understood that each spouse's opposite number in the other couple brought into their lives missing aspects of what they desired and acted as a stabilizing, rather than an unsettling, influence in their marriages.

Frances and Jack were very interested in the apartment above ours because of the shortage of modern apartments at reasonable prices in the Village. The reality about apartments in Greenwich Village was that many were substandard. Some of the tenements had no bathtubs so that residents had to use a public bathhouse on Hudson Street, finally built for them after much political agitation. When one thinks of the poor housing conditions some of the immigrants endured it's a wonder that there wasn't a greater manifestation of tensions between the haves and the have-nots. That there wasn't is evidence of the laissez-faire attitude of each group.

Jack and Frances's daughter Cissie was a very pretty young woman who had a bad case of acne and wanted to be a model. She had large eyes and a square chin that was very much in vogue in those days. After attending a modeling school and regularly going to a skin doctor for her acne, she'd make the rounds of modeling agencies each week, but with little luck. I'm sure I didn't add to her self-confidence by telling her every single time I saw her that her skin was looking better. But she always accepted my little girl comments graciously without self-consciousness.

Her brother Jack had served in Italy during World War II. Whenever we saw him he would invariably act out stories about shooting down the enemy hiding in houses along the streets of the towns he fought in. He made rifle noises with his mouth that were quite realistic or at least good enough to keep my grandmother, who didn't understand a word he said, laughing at his sounds. We all joined in the laughter too. Only once do I remember hearing something that made me understand what a serious situation the war was. The mother of one of my friends was castigating Lucille, my playmate, for wasting food. Her mouth was drawn tight and her eyebrows knit together as she said, "There are people who don't have enough food. Your cousin overseas in the Army would love to be eating what you're wasting."

When I was growing up, the Waverly movie house on Sixth Avenue was not the art house, the IFC—Infiltrate Film Center—it is today, but rather it was the neighborhood movie house, which my aunt, uncle and their daughter attended three times a week, no matter what the film. 'A' films then came to movie houses for two or three days when it would move on and new films— double features—would arrive. The double feature would show one 'A' film with first-rate actors, like Humphrey Bogart and Alan Ladd, and a 'B' film with lesser actors, whose names no longer live on, and less compelling scripts. Later my aunt and her daughter, who was my godmother, became devotees of the soaps on television. These replaced movie going.

As much as I regarded my aunt and her daughter as exemplars of the hospitality of Martha and Mary of the

Bible, when the soaps came on at 2:30, it was their time and guests be hanged. They had both worked at the Rogers Peet factory. My aunt put in linings to men's suits and coats. She brought long scraps of leftover linings home with her. My grandmother promptly set about making hooked rugs for our summerhouse. This same sense of thrift made her save the string from pastry boxes that she rolled into large balls. Twelve such balls were her 'legacy' to me when I married.

My aunt and her daughter blessed the Ladies Garment Workers of America for the pensions they received in their retirement years. While small compared to today, their pensions satisfied their needs and they never seemed to worry about money, eschewing food on sale and buying what they desired. Nor to the end did they ever stint on hospitality. It was always a feast there with chocolates, three kinds of cookies, pears and apples that they skinned for us, various nuts, and hot chocolate—or when we were older, vermouth—to drink.

My brother and I attended movies together. At Saturday matinees we'd arrive 'whenever' as was the custom then, not necessarily at the beginning of the film since movie plots were generally much simpler and we could fill in whatever we had missed at the beginning. Of course, we'd then watch the beginning of the movie until we came to the part we had walked in on and could correct any misconceptions this mode of viewing might have caused us. But we were rarely wrong in our surmises.

Our parents warned us not to sit in the balcony or near old men. For twenty-five cents we'd watch the movie while munching on a five-cent box of candy. Although in many ways this was a simpler time—by the time I was in sixth grade, I was allowed to ride the bus uptown with a friend to go to museums like the Museum of Natural History— nonetheless my parents and the nuns warned us about the dangers that a city holds. They said we should hide our wallets deep in our pockets and keep our hands on them while riding in the bus. M mother told me to walk on the other side of the street from the Mills Hotel on Bleecker Street. I didn't have to be told that twice. According to my father, it was a fifty-cent flophouse where drunks slept for the night. The men could be seen staggering in and out of the building at all hours of the day. They were unshaven and they muttered various oaths and curse words as they reeled and barged along the sidewalk.

The building itself was rather nice looking—on the outside—with an imposing stone entrance. Later a developer saw its possibilities, cleaned the outside stone, restoring it to its original white, re-did the inner courtyard into an atrium and re-named the building the Atruim, now a high-priced residence.

When my parents finally allowed me to walk to school by myself in fourth grade, they weren't at all confident of my abilities to navigate the city so they had my grandmother tail me. Their final injunction to me was not to accept candy from strange men. Being unable to imagine what danger such an action held as well as hoping someone *would* offer me free candy, the scenario I envisioned was that I would accept the candy but then not go wherever that person wanted me to go.

As a young teenager, I ventured out of the Village more and more, often to attend the Metropolitan Opera, standing room only for $1.65 for the Saturday matinee at the Old Met. One time the friend with whom I most often attended was able to obtain tickets for us for the radio broadcast with Milton Cross. I always read the synopsis of the operas in a book edited by Cross and in the days before suprascript, I'd buy the libretto of the opera for that day's performance and study it. I'd memorize the opening lines of the arias in Italian or French to better follow the story. In doing this, I was introduced to standard Italian, a language that, to my great regret, I never studied in school. My high school didn't offer it and in college my advisor discouraged me from taking it. But those arias made me understand in what way most words in my grandmother's dialect were related to standard Italian. I never did learn how two words, *iudo* for 'I went' and *saccio* for 'I know' were related to standard Italian. Just recently I learned that *saccio* for 'I know' was the form Dante used.

When I was a college student, I enjoyed going with dates to the White Horse Tavern. Not at all architecturally interesting, it's nonetheless noteworthy for the unpleasant fact that Dylan Thomas died after a long night of drinking there. What I liked about the White Horse was that it opened up a wider world to me: my date and I would share tables with other couples and often met artists, writers and cub reporters at the *New York Times,* always willing to talk on a variety of topics. Though we were not of the world of the arts, we had access to it and that, for then, was sufficient.

A decade later when I almost thirty and living in the twin cities of Champaign-Urbana, I had occasion to meet John Cage at parties as well as authors and other artists in residence that year at the University of Illinois' sesquicentennial celebrations. What struck me about some of those artists was their arch relationship to their work. While I could understand Cage's desire to break new ground, his random mode of composing never made me his fan. On the other hand, artist Leo Leoni's offer to take me mushrooming (an invitation I didn't avail myself of) made me a fan of his for life. And who could resist Ferdinand, the poet?

Taking leave of Greenwich Village, such a unique locale that nurtured me as well as expanded my horizons is always fraught with emotion. But perhaps I've come full circle: I live in Cambridge around the corner from the William James House—one of the brothers who lived not far away from my natal home in Greenwich Village. And perhaps as Henry fretted, the immigrants *did* conquer New York, but not in the way he feared.

Chapter 3

Fumbling Towards Peace and Trembling

Our neighbor Millie stood in profile next to my mother in our narrow hallway. She lumbered towards the door of my grandmother's bedroom. "Teresina, my daughter's sick...I'm so worried about her." Her voice was pinched and shrill as if it might ascend to an upper register and not come down again. "I don't want to get sick myself, the way I am." She caressed her stomach and left her hand there, her fingers rising and falling in a soft lulling rhythm that belied her anxiety. "...Such a high fever. Can you help her..." she hunched forward as if what she had to say needed to be whispered privately, "Can you help her...get better?"

She furrowed her brow as she addressed my grandmother. A sister-in-law of Jimmy the Butcher, Millie had been married a long time before having her first child. A pretty woman in a pleasant sort of way with regular features and a ready smile, she was now pregnant for a second time. She and her husband were one of the younger couples in our apartment building in the Italian section of Greenwich Village. Being of a later generation than my parents, I was drawn to their more modern ways. They treated me as if I were their equal—not as a child who should be seen and not heard.

My grandmother was sitting in her bedroom, saying her rosary by the double windows. The rosary beads spilled into the lap of her dress, making a slight depression in her skirt. No lights were on. The Venetian blinds were nearly closed, obscuring the building next door, twenty feet away with no windows interrupting its brick wall. My grandmother's darkened profile was silhouetted against the white blinds. She stood up and slipped her black rosary into her pocket, put on her wire-rim glasses, and walked over to Millie.

"Go get me Linda's barrette," she said to Millie in Italian, "and I'll pray for her tonight...at the right time. Don't you worry. She'll get better. Such a nice little girl... Nice-a, nice-a," she added in broken English. She gave a little laugh and shuffled in her open-backed slippers to her chair to resume her rosary. Millie returned a wan smile, wrung her hands, and nodded slowly. I was surprised that, despite her more modern ways, Millie believed in my grandmother's powers.

Later I saw my grandmother, sitting in silhouette by her bedroom windows once more, the room dark again, and holding the barrette out in front of her while she murmured some prayers. Sibilant sounds sneaked from between her taut lips.

"How does Nana holding the barrette help Millie's daughter?" I interrupted my mother, who was listening to Lux Radio Theater in the living room. The lamp brightened the dark painting on the wall of a wind-tossed ship at sea. Three framed black silhouettes of my mother, my brother, and me hung opposite it. My mother's plants smothered the top of a delicate end table—spider plants, pothos, and philodendron. The schefflera stood nearby in a flowered ceramic pot on the floor.

"Nana's praying over the barrette because she needs something that the sick person's worn, close to where the sickness is. I asked her once to tell me the prayers she said to cure people, but she said if she told me, she'd lose her power. She said she could only tell me the words at midnight, but she's never has...Nana is good, but she's not as powerful as Camille's grandmother, Serafina. She used to charge two dollars when other *fatturas* were charging fifty cents. Oh, Serafina was powerful," my mother emphasized. "She could even heal broken bones."

A few days later, I was crossing Greenwich Street where cars emptied into Sixth Avenue at a forty-five degree angle while traffic from Eighth Street barreled into the avenue from the opposite direction. Jaywalkers skirted the cars turning off both streets. Long shadows hung across the broad intersection. At five o'clock in the afternoon people rushed down the stairs from work to the Sixth Avenue Subway at Fourth Street. Others hustled about avoiding pedestrians going in and out of stores along the way—the

Five and Dime, the bank, a bookstore.

I crossed Sixth and walked down to Waverly Place, where a crowd had gathered by the lamppost at the corner. Four or five-dozen adults milled about, listening to the speaker, a short man who wagged his finger in a stabbing motion. He was talking about peace. I was for that. His voice rose over the screeching of cars and the bustle of people hurrying by. I stayed to listen. Right away a middle-aged woman in a brown suit approached me, the heels of her shoes clicking against the sidewalk. She smiled at me. Hugging a clipboard tightly to her chest, she asked me to add my name to the signatures already there: It was a peace petition the group intended to send to President Truman regarding the Korean War. I was flattered that she approached *me* when she could have asked any number of grown-ups. I signed, happy to be part of the adult doings.

That night I sat on our rose sofa reading *The News*. I stared at a diagram in the newspaper. It pictured a map of the center of Manhattan as well as our neighborhood to the south. It marked a direct hit on the Empire State Building and then drew dark wavy lines in concentric circles expanding out from there, showing the radius of damage resulting from an atomic bomb. It scared me to look at it, because if the communists dropped an A-bomb on mid-town New York, we would be right in the center of the destruction. I shuddered.

The next day as usual at three o'clock, my mother was waiting for me on the park bench where a little group of students' mothers sat chatting while they watched their children play. I left my books with her; then I lined up behind Geraldine and Judy who were poised to jump into a game of double-Dutch jump rope. When we tired of that, we chalked in a hopscotch rectangle on the sidewalk and searched for something to use for a patsy. Geraldine found a flattened piece of aluminum from one of our previous games and we began. My mother called to me. "Come on, Carol. Let's go. It's time to do our errands and go home."

The following Saturday I again accompanied my mother on her errands. She needed a new rat for her bun. She had changed her hairstyle from the upsweep style of hair framing the head, so popular during the war, to a chignon at the back. As we walked towards Waverly Place, I saw the peace people again. My mother twisted her body towards me and turned her head towards the crowd. "Some peace makers!" she said. "They're a communist front."

For a moment, as I stared at the peace people, my eyes saw double. I had signed a communist-front petition. Would the government snare me in their round up because I sympathized with communists? Maybe my handwriting would save me. The president would know I was just a grammar school kid and that I didn't mean to overthrow the government. The vehemence of my mother's voice made my knees go numb, but I kept walking. I didn't want her to think I was dumb enough to fall for a communist front organization.

When World War II ended, I was six. For me, war meant sitting in our kitchen peeling the thin foil sheet from my gum wrapper and saving it for one of the kids who collected such bits and loaded them into his red wagon along with old newspapers. Or telling the same joke over and over, "What did Hitler say when he took off his boots?"

"I smell de-feat."

Or going with my grandmother to the dark basement church on the First Friday of the month to hear Mass and light a candle in a red glass holder, shimmering like a ruby in the darkness, the only light in the shadowy, nearly deserted church; hearing the coin offering drop in the slot nearby, clinking in the stillness. My grandmother and I bowed our heads and prayed for her two grandsons, my cousins, who were serving in the war. One was in Oklahoma and the other, who had volunteered and was underage to boot, was overseas.

But for this current war in 1951—or more technically this police action in Korea—I was, if no more cognizant of what war was like or that communist fronts existed, beginning to become aware of how scared Americans were of communists. I saw the Rosenbergs' photos in the newspaper.

My father told me that there were limits to free speech: you couldn't advocate the violent overthrow of our government as the communists did. For him it was a straightforward matter of being against the law. The Smith Act had seen to that.

The Rosenbergs had been convicted of giving secrets to the Russians and I had gone and signed a communist-front peace petition. I feared that I had helped the communists by signing their peace petition. I was in fear and trembling, wondering what would happen to me.

My mother wasn't the only one concerned about Communists. A few years earlier in 1948, the American and the Italian governments encouraged Italian Americans to write to their relatives in Italy to tell them not to vote Communist. One of my uncles who could write Italian mailed our relatives a letter, urging them to vote against the Communists. Since the war had devastated Italy, and the South of Italy had never been in great shape to begin with, impoverished Italians might be tempted to vote for the Communists. But that was Italy. This was America.

I knew about the poverty in Italy because I had seen photos of our relatives. They were skinny and poorly dressed. They stood in front of a crumbling farmhouse. Ever since the end of the war, my family had sent my grandmother's sister, widowed with six daughters and her son dead, huge packages of clothes: women's dresses, blouses, skirts, coats, even an old fur one, men's suits, shoes, hats; whatever my mother could collect not only from our extended family but also from our neighbors. Nothing was turned away. My mother figured that whatever the six girls and their mother couldn't use, like the evening blouse with spaghetti straps and the men's suits, they might be able to sell for something else and not vote Communist.

As for the woman with the petition, I resented her for taking advantage of my youth and I was annoyed at myself that I wasn't sufficiently grown up to know the full story. My head was spinning. Senator McCarthy was harassing people for just knowing communists. I saw him on TV banging his fist on the table, his voice sounding as sharp and tough as the leaves of an old artichoke. Would the government think I knew communists too because I had signed the petition?

My father's perspective on communism had nothing to do with his being a Catholic for he was anti-clerical. In contrast, my eighth grade teacher, Sister Ellen, who was Irish American, made a distinction between godless communism and the kind she practiced as a nun.

Sister Ellen liked dramatic statements. They were part of a repertory that she repeated often with the exact same inflection and timing, standing at the side of her desk, pretending to be correcting a misstatement. "The God of the atom bomb," she would begin after one of our atomic bomb drills forced us to hide under our desks, "The God, I mean," she would quickly correct herself, "of the atom. Man made the bomb." Then she would whirl away from the side of her desk, stand behind it and continue her lesson.

Or when she made a distinction between atheistic communism, which she abhorred, and a form of communism that the nuns practiced on a smaller scale as part of their vow to God of poverty. "We don't own anything individually here at school," she'd say. "We live communally and receive from Mother Superior whatever we need. I don't hate communism," she'd conclude. "I hate atheistic communism." And thus she thought—correctly as it happened—that we would remember the distinctions. Imparting such 'wisdom' was one of her ways of preparing us for adulthood.

For at least a month I held my breath when I heard my father's key in the door, I would rush down the long hallway to greet him, but mostly to see if he had brought in any mail for me. I wondered if the communists or the government had sent me a letter. I had given my address on the petition. I was sure the dreaded communists would haunt me to work for them or that the U. S. government would arrest me.

I fretted every night and started going to Mass before school. I lit a candle as I had with my grandmother during the war. I lingered, watching the flame crest and then fall. As I breathed in the oily fragrance of the melting wax pooling at the bottom, I decided to ask my grandmother to pray over my pen, without telling her why. Maybe her powers would be able to protect me.

I stood by our living room window, staring at the sky

and biting my lower lip, wondering what the authorities would do to me. What kind of a fix had I gotten myself into? What had I done to my country? But no letter came—and President Truman never called me to appear before the House Un-American Activities Committee. Perhaps my grandmother's prayers had helped me after all.

In the fall of 1951, I went off to high school, St. Lawrence Academy, a renovated brownstone on East 84th Street on the Upper East Side, where educating eighty-three girls was far too few to be stimulating. The Sisters of Charity order, which I had had in grammar school, gave scholarships to their high schools to the top student in class and that's how I came to be at St. Lawrence. The Upper East Side was not the sort of neighborhood where you'd see communist fronts talking peace on the streets.

That year our high school nuns were urging our parents to make a command appearance to hear Louis Budenz speak. He was a former communist, having left the Party after WWII. He had been the editor of the *Daily Worker*. Subsequently, Budenz had returned to Catholicism and now traveled around the country to inform Americans of all the communists who had infiltrated the government. I handed my parents the flyer with details about his talk.

When the scheduled night of the lecture arrived, my parents and I sat in my high school auditorium. It was full. A short, trim man with graying black hair and intense eyes, stood at the edge of the small stage. Louis Budenz wore a black suit and white shirt. He gave example after example of government infiltration as we all sat in the auditorium. His never-ending catalogue of communists in government was frightening. How had such a thing occurred? Had I helped the communists by signing that peace petition a year earlier? On the way home, my parents were silent—whether from fear or suspicion as to his motives, I'll never know. Some said Budenz changed his tune to save his skin and that the whole thing was a red herring. I'll never know what the truth of that situation was and I began to see that complexity touched all human undertakings.

My grandmother's prayers, which remained secret, did cure Millie's daughter. At high school, the atomic bomb drills, which had been instituted during my last years in grammar school, continued all through the year.

Though I didn't sign any more peace petitions, we girls were now discussing McCarthy. My classmate Mimi and I agreed that McCarthy's methods were indefensible in a democracy. The fear at the time I had signed the peace petition, and which had grown geometrically since, infected the whole country. Such infections, however, were beyond the powers of my grandmother to cure, just as love of one's children couldn't always be controlled rationally either.

I learned more about current events to avoid further stumblings into adulthood. It seemed to me that the country was behind the war and against communism and people like McCarthy would use these attitudes to their own advantage. I also learned that emotions brought with them a certain amount of chaos, if not on a level of the great tragedies for ordinary people like me, nonetheless with enough power to upset lives.

Chapter 4

Long Beach, Ancestors & Other Things

I was very young when World War II ended and I didn't know what war meant. For me, it was a matter of being mesmerized by the searchlights illuminating the night sky, their beams going round and round, intersecting every so often; they seemed a variation on the bright lights of Broadway. To shield me, my parents never told me the beams searched for enemy planes. War meant pulling down the green shades for a blackout one night during those years. It meant rushing uptown when my mother heard she could get both meat and sugar there; or accompanying her on her search for nylon stockings.

Whenever stockings arrived at a Gimbel's or Orbach's, the word got around and women flocked to Thirty-fourth Street or Fourteenth. This particular day my mother and I joined the long queue at Gimbel's.

"Hold my hat and go stand over there," my mother directed, pointing off to the side of the line. My mother often got on line twice, once wearing her hat pulled down on her forehead with me beside her and the next time hat off, with me to the side waiting, forlorn and alone, lost amidst a crowd of anxious women pressing forward. My mother's subterfuges and disguises embarrassed me.

The only newspaper photos I remember about the war were of Germans carrying suitcases full of money to buy bread. At the age of six, when the war in Europe ended, I didn't understand that their money was now all but worthless. But the photo struck me as the other side of endings and beginnings.

In grammar school years later, I would learn about the A-bomb being dropped on Japan. And years after that, I would meet Sir Hugh Taylor, who had worked on the Manhattan Project to develop the bomb. He was visiting Brown University, where my then husband taught. For some reason I no longer remember, we were asked to take him to dinner, which along with a bachelor friend, we did. It was a dark little restaurant in downtown Providence and the four of us shared a quiet intimate dinner. We three, of course, shared a natural curiosity about getting the inside story to the Manhattan Project. Sir Hugh was a soft-spoken man, who answered our questions about the project in a direct manner. His response to the rationale behind dropping the bomb on civilians was the familiar one of its having saved hundreds of thousands of Allied lives in wartime.

When the war ended in August 1945, we were at our summerhouse on Long Island. Long Beach was just thirty miles from New York City, but it took over an hour to get there. The Long Island Expressway hadn't yet been built and so our black Chevy, which we babied all through the war, limped along Sunrise Highway with all its congestion from commercial stores lining the way. Such roads were hardly like the highways of today. In those days, the legal limit was thirty-five miles an hour—forty-five on major roads. So our trip took roughly an hour—longer if we had to wait on the final leg of our journey for the bridge tender to raise the drawbridge for the passing of a sailboat with a tall mast.

Long Beach was a city sort of beach community with an East End, mostly Jewish and year-round living, and a summertime West End, a mixture of Jews and Catholics and a smattering of Protestants. The Loop Parkway connected the eastern border of the island to Jones Beach, the 2,143-acre marine park with six and half miles of ocean that Robert Moses built.

Long Beach is a barrier island off the south shore of Long Island, less than a half-mile wide at the West End with three parallel streets—Beach, Park and Sea View—running along its length. Cross streets alternate between wide and narrow widths, the wide streets having a divider in the middle planted with blue hydrangeas.

The Rockaway Indians sold the area to the colonists in 1643. When Congress established a lifesaving station there to rescue sailors whose boats had run aground or were beached, Long Beach finally developed as a place to live. In 1880, Austin Corbin was the first to try to develop the land. He partnered with the Long Island Railroad to finance the laying of track from Lynbrook to Long Beach, but was unsuccessful in his attempt to develop the island as a resort. Finally in 1906, William Reynolds bought the oceanfront from private owners and, in 1907, the rest of the island from the town of Hempstead. He built a boardwalk along the ocean and homes and hotels. To live up to his building of Long Beach as the "Riviera of the East," he required every building to be constructed in a Mediterranean style with white stucco walls and red tile roofs. He further stipulated that only white Anglo-Saxon Protestants could live there. The irony of Mediterranean style housing for Anglo-Saxons was obviously lost on Reynolds. When his corporation went bankrupt in 1919, these restrictions were lifted and Long Beach was open to all.

But Long Beach remained mainly a white community. What blacks there were lived behind the railroad station. When I was growing up we would take the bus there and then walk to the library a few blocks away. We saw the unemployed, and sometimes drunk, black men lolling about those back streets during the day. We never went there at night.

I was acquainted with two Negro girls, as we said in those days. One was Helen, who lived with her white mother in a basement apartment and insisted she was an American Indian. We believed her because we had never seen an Indian anyway. The other was a girl, L., my age, who worked as an 'au pair' for a family who rented a house for a month during the summer. She would hang out with me and my friends on the evenings that she was free. We talked about the typical girl interests we had, such as who our favorite male singers were and which ones we swooned over. Unlike the days at my first school, Our Lady of Mercy, we no longer split along Irish/Italian lines of arguing the merits of Frank Sinatra and Bing Crosby. By our teen years we could relinquish such narrow ethnocentric loyalties because there was an array of Italian-American singers to choose from. But when we asked L. who her favorite male singer was, she answered, "Nat King Cole." As much as we all liked Nat King Cole, none of us had mentioned him. We could enjoy his singing but we couldn't swoon over him. We nodded knowingly at her choice.

In the 1920s the new town of Long Beach attracted wealthy businessmen and entertainers, such as dancers Vernon and Irene Castle who performed at the theater called Castels by the Sea. Jose Ferrer, Mae West, and Zero Mostel were some of the actors who performed at local theaters. Jack Dempsey, Florenz Ziegfeld, James Cagney, Clara Bow and John Barrymore lived in Long Beach for a time. John Dos Passos in *The Big Money* mentions weekends spent in Long Beach in the 1920s.

When I lived there in the nineteen forties and fifties, Jack Teagarden's family had a summerhouse there. I knew his daughter, Dru Ann, who attended my grammar school, St. Joseph Academy. She was a few years younger than I. You could tell she came from a show business family because by second grade, her hair had been dyed blonde. The ever-tolerant nuns never commented on it.

Built as summer cottages, the white-shingled houses in the West End often followed two or three standard layouts. But ours, near the bay, was unique as far as I could tell: an enclosed front porch the width of the house, then a living room/dining room divided by pillars atop a half wall on either side of a central archway. The tiny kitchen was at the back with three bedrooms off to the side and an open back porch. Before hot water was connected to the outdoor shower (we had only a bathtub inside), we rinsed off in the shower's cold water as fast as we could upon returning from the beach.

Very few houses had garages, the community having been developed well before cars were common. Before the season began, my mother, brother and I—since my father was working—took the Long Island Railroad to Long Beach, our excitement mounting as the conductor called out the towns of Valley Stream, Oceanside, and Island Park before we arrived at the last stop. "Long Beach," he'd call, his voice extending the 'Long' and falling at the 'Beach.'

Then we took a taxi from the station to open the house for the summer. This involved our waiting for the plumber to turn on the water. My mother busied herself airing out the house and carrying pillows from the sofa, chairs and beds outside, into the sunshine. I climbed on the white picket fence out back and balanced myself on its narrow ledge, walking past neighbors' yards. The air was fresh and crisp. My mother and I cut ivy from our front yard and, as our heads bent together over the pots, we arranged the greenery. We hung the pots from the room dividers so that the ivy spilled over in graceful profusion.

The kitchen still had a wooden icebox since the manufacture of consumer goods was not a priority during the war. Frank, the iceman, slid the ice into the top section of the icebox. This had a hole at the back, attached to a pipe, for the melt to drain into a bottom well that my mother emptied regularly. She placed the food in a compartment beneath the ice section.

"Is he here yet? Can you see him down the block?" I asked my brother Tom one hot July day as we craned our necks to see if Frank the iceman's truck was meandering along the street. Along with our friends we kids eagerly waited for Frank to deliver a block of ice, cut to the weight my mother ordered. His truck finally wheezed into view.

"Hi, Frank," Tom and I said in chorus.

Frank smiled at us. He was a genial, somewhat portly, though muscular, man with brown curly hair. "How are you kids today?"

"Hot," we answered again in unison. Frank smiled at us once more, removed the canvas covering the large blocks of ice and cut a piece on the wood floor of his open-backed truck to the weight my mother ordered. As he cut, we squinted at the splinters of ice flying about. As soon as Frank hoisted the cut block on his shoulder and lumbered towards our backdoor, we ignored our mother's warnings about the evils of the chemicals used in the ice—ice was water, we reasoned—and we snagged slivers from the back of his truck, its wooden panels dripping water onto the road below. We grabbed as many succulent morsels as we could, stuffing them into our mouths. We sucked and slurped the bits and pieces as he and his ice truck moved on to his next delivery.

Off Park Street was the bay where we learned to swim, moving from a four-year-old's version of swimming—each stroke ending on the sand beneath us in the shallow water—to the real thing when my father, without my knowing it, let go of me and I didn't sink. We spent our morning hours at the bay, swimming, splashing and riding on discarded black inner tubes. One July day I was floating along the gentle waves. Not wanting to lazy about any longer, I jumped off the tube. I waited to touch bottom, but that didn't happen; instead I went down, down, down. What was going on?

I finally bobbed up. Startled, I opened my mouth and swallowed water. I sputtered it out only to let more water in. I went down a second time and swallowed even more yet again, choking and gasping. On the third dunk I felt the lifeguard's arms around me. He scooped me up, kept my head above water to my relief, and brought me to shore. People gathered around me with my mother in the lead while I, still dazed, coughed up gallons of salty water through my nose and mouth—it felt like I had swallowed the whole bay.

"Are you all right?" my mother asked. "What happened out there? You were so far out."

"I don't know. I guess I slipped off my tube," I sputtered, not wanting her to know that I wasn't aware that I was in over my head.

My mother and I gathered up our things—her chair and the blanket. We brought no towels because my mother believed in having us 'sun-dry' ourselves to lessen her laundry. We never had a washing machine in Long Beach and, before laundromats came into vogue there, my mother did all the laundry by hand, rubbing our clothes against a washboard—not that there was a lot of clothing to wash since we spent at least half the day in bathing suits.

We walked home from the bay. I was quiet during the short walk, but by the next day I was ready to go back into the water.

The beach there was dotted with houses priced during the war for the taking. My father wasn't interested in any of them since he thought the little beaches at the bay would be noisy nuisances.

Off Sea View Lane was the majestic ocean with miles of white sand, where we went in the afternoon to try our hand at riding waves or, in my case, just floating over them before they broke, my breathing magnified like an echo chamber from the effect of my bathing cap pressed against my ears. Still wild, the ocean had not yet been tamed by jetties.

Because of its location on the water, Long Beach residents were concerned about German submarines hiding off their coastline. They were aware that in January of 1942 U-boat 123 had sunk the *Norness* sixty miles off Montauk Point at the end of Long Island. The next evening the same German submarine was seen sailing westward along the south shore of Long Island towards New York City, where nets and shore batteries protected the throat of it harbor. The submarine fortunately never reached the City because as they passed by the Rockaway shore, which was not very distant from Long Beach, the crew, not having detailed charts of the area and not knowing of the southward curve of the Rockaways, almost beached themselves on the nearby shores.

Jones Beach also played an important role in the war effort. It was one of three Radio Direction Finding Stations in the New York-New Jersey area. The station homed in on the Enigma-coded messages transmitted by the German U-boats. The Enigma-code machine looked like a typewriter, but it had a set of rotators that scrambled the letters inconsistently on a regular basis, making it almost impossible to break. But four Polish mathematicians succeeded in breaking the code, an invaluable accomplishment for the Allies.

The first autumn after we bought our house in the spring of 1944, a hurricane had caused the ocean on the south side of the island and the bay on the north to meet. We drove down to see if our house was still there. It was, although a good number of houses—those right on the bay and the ocean—weren't. They had been swept away and dumped in unlikely spots, lopsided in their landing like a tinker toy a child had knocked over. In its disarray, the town was a child's delight. All structures and, by extension, all authority had been toppled. We explored at will, poking into abandoned homes, swearing to our parents that we hadn't and reveling in these small acts of anarchy, free from parental supervision, and marveling at and excited by the destruction.

My father often smelled of cigarettes. Not even the odor of salt air could mask it. A chain smoker who knew smoking did him no good, he tried—several times—to give them up. Once he tried cold turkey. Another time he tried a gradual withdrawal, smoking mentholated filter cigarettes. Next he tried not inhaling. Nothing seemed to work. Finally, and very self-consciously, he tried a cigarette holder á la FDR. To my father and to most of us, a cigarette holder was an upper-class accoutrement. But even this was given up and he made his peace with cigarettes by telling himself that he'd rather give up the five years of his life that this habit would cost him than the daily pleasure that smoking gave him.

Whenever my father was dressing to go out, he laid out two ties on the bed and asked me to pick the one I liked best, as I did this day.

"Hm-m-m, the gold tie with the dots or the navy with the stripes," I mused, glancing up at my father as I lifted the ties off the rose bedspread. I hung first one, then the other on my index finger. I studied the ties by the light of the window. I moved to my father's side and put each tie up against his jacket.

"I like the navy blue with maroon stripes," I announced at last. My father smiled down at me, took the tie from my hand and turned towards the mirror. I sat on the bed, swinging my legs while I watched him knot his tie. I felt as I always did: that he valued my opinion and loved me, as I did him. When I was little, I followed him everywhere, even to the bathroom.

My feelings towards my mother were more complicated due to the family story surrounding my birth and the way she always seemed to fault me whenever my brother Tom and I argued. The story was that, in delivering me my mother almost died from blood poisoning. In addition, her legs were paralyzed for three months after my birth. This latter condition, the doctor told her, would be permanent. It was only her will to walk again, she said, that reversed the situation.

The telling of this story always left me with the impression that I wasn't cherished; that my coming into the world had caused my mother much pain, suffering and bother. Although it was also said that her blood poisoning was due to her having waited two days to tell the doctor that her water had broken, because she didn't want to inconvenience him, this part of the tale did little to dispel my feelings that *I* was a nuisance at birth and a nuisance still. Even my father's story about the nurse, who, when readying me to go home from the hospital, hugged me and said how pretty I was, couldn't alleviate my feelings of being unwanted.

Part of my 'birth story' was connected to the larger 'survival myth' that flourished on my mother's side of the family: of their having survived the boat crossing to America and their subsequent poverty from which both my parents rose by dint of their efforts. In that context, I understood later that the circumstances of my birth were part of a series of events that needed to be overcome and conquered. This insight changed my perspective somewhat. It was part of an 'immigrant triumphant' story, not unlike the American 'exceptionalism' myth which reached its peak at the end of the nineteenth century.

The 'immigrant triumphant' story had several parts. One of the stories—a female "John Bunyon" tale, Italian-style—emphasized the physical strength and powers of endurance of the immigrants. In our family the storyteller demonstrated the myth in two ways: one contrasted the manner in which birth occurred in Italy and in America. In Italy the pregnant woman gave birth in the fields and then went straight back to work. This was contrasted with the American way of giving birth, which was treated as a sickness, where the women were hospitalized, thus emphasizing the weakness of the Americans as compared with the hardy Italians.

The other mythic story involved the work my grandmother did upon first coming to America. Again the story emphasized the strength of the immigrant: my grandmother not only found a job for herself within a week of landing, but she found a job that men typically did, namely working a large steam press in a clothing factory. Such strength suggested that we, the descendents of these immigrants—my mother's generation included— were mere mortals compared to the superhuman demands that the immigrants addressed so successfully. Their heroic behavior had made our life of ease possible. Implied in that was the paradoxical notion that in our ease we nonetheless partook of our ancestors' heroism.

Another part of the story included my grandmother's taking in laundry at night after working all day. At some point, my mother told me, my mother's brother, Louie, insisted that his mother not continue this work, which was done in a large laundry tub.

Later my mother told me of another enterprise that my grandmother undertook for extra cash: she made her own wine and sold it by the glassful to single men in their apartment building. This hardly seemed a Bunyonesque display of strength. My mother must have noticed my shock at learning that my grandmother bootlegged wine because she added, with a chuckle at my naiveté, "In those days during Prohibition...things were different." I got the impression that selling wine was partly a social custom among people with little discretionary income, founded as much on the sociability of the winemaker as the quality of the wine.

According to my mother, my widowed grandmother was a lively, sought after woman. One man in her apartment building wanted to marry my grandmother. Again my mother registered my surprise: my grandmother was no beauty with her bulbous nose and stout body. But my mother stressed that Nana had an infectious laugh and an endless supply of funny stories in rhyme, told in dialect, using words that in themselves sounded humorous. Too, she was energetic and a hard worker, qualities that would recommend someone in any society, but especially an immigrant one.

My godmother Lillie told me that in her younger days my grandmother was good-looking. This may be true since each of her three children was very good looking: Louie was a handsome six-footer, Rose had a lush beauty with her olive complexion, and my mother was the double of the movie star, Mary Pickford.

An impetus to my grandmother's coming to America was that a second marriage had been arranged with her dead husband's relative. Sight unseen, she crossed the Atlantic to find that her assumption that he would be a good man like her husband was false. After they married, she learned that he was a mean-spirited drunkard who would take his own three children out for ice cream, but leave her three children home. Again her son eventually intervened and urged his mother to leave this man, but before she did, she and her children suffered under his abuse, both physical and psychological.

He was the superintendent of the apartment building they lived in. He insisted that they all eat with him at suppertime in the furnace room as he tended the coal-burning furnace. Practically on her deathbed, my mother told me this haunting detail and how she and Rose would sit up 'guarding' their mother to be sure she was not abused. My mother wondered why such a thought was going round and round in her head at this time. So much silence had marked the existence of this husband—for years I didn't know that my grandmother had entered into a second marriage—that I wasn't surprised that these thoughts invaded my mother's head.

Many years later I learned more about my mother's relationship to my grandmother. My grandmother, having been widowed when pregnant with my mother, unsuccessfully tried to abort her. My mother was aware of this and remained an unwanted child throughout her life. She could never please my grandmother who was often prickly and argumentative with her. When she was really angry with my mother about some squabble they had, she would threaten to move out and live with her other daughter. This was an extremely effective manipulation since, in our neighborhood, it would have been a dreadful disgrace to the adult child for a mother to leave her daughter's home.

My grandmother was an equal opportunity vituperative type, who picked on her other daughter as well, but not as frequently as she did with my mother whose very proximity, living together as they did, caused some of the problems. Two women together in the kitchen in our household often resulted in endless bickering. To avoid the worst of the wrangles, I rarely went in there when my mother and grandmother were preparing a meal together. Coming from her Mediterranean background, my grandmother never spoke harshly to her son who was the favored child who could do no wrong. Nonetheless, the subsequent knowledge of my grandmother's actions didn't affect my relationship with her for I had known only her tenderness.

In a way, my grandmother's treatment of my mother caused my mother's mode of treating me and at the same time it was my grandmother's treatment of me through which she redeemed herself. Her being a widow with three children was responsible for her dire action as well as her reason for immigrating to America. I can only conclude that good and bad effects seem to flow from one event, balancing the eternal struggle between good and evil. Or at least so it has appeared a couple of times in my life.

Although my grandmother's first husband owned a

gristmill, when he died three months before my mother was born, my grandmother found herself unable to collect payment for her services. According to my mother, women in the Italy of that time were dismissed as businesswomen. So my grandmother finally immigrated in 1907 when my mother was four years old.

My grandmother's now buried where many of the immigrants were buried, in Calvary Cemetery—a vast tract of land that spans lower Manhattan and the adjoining part of Brooklyn. It's as large as some towns with its own map—larger even than my grandmother's homctown—with the stones marking the dead spreading out as far as the eye can see with its chaotic jumble dotting every inch of the land. It is there where all my ancestors lie.

As long as I was in the company of older kids—either my brother Tom or two older girls, whom my family knew from the city (and whom my parents thought were responsible young women)—I had a great deal of freedom to roam. My parents thought of this small town with few cars during the day and no crime—doors were left unlocked—as not needing the vigilance they practiced in the city.

One sunny day before the beginning of the season, while my mother bustled about getting the house ready for the summer, my brother and I and the two older girls, Roseanne and Marguerite, walked over to the bay, called Reynold's Channel. No one was on the beach at that time of year. Someone had left an old battered rowboat in need of a coat of paint moored to the remains of a wooden pier, its ragged pilings worn smooth and pointing towards the sky. Half a dozen such pilings stood forlorn out from the shoreline with several loose planks stretching across the ramshackle pier. The neglected boat had two oars lying crisscrossed on its center seat.

Without thinking twice, the four of us leaped across the boards and hopped into the boat. It rocked dangerously in response. Once steadied and seated, we untied it and began to row, two to an oar. The tide was with us and we cut across the water quickly, enjoying the sun on our backs and the salt on our faces. The horizon seemed an infinite distance from us with no limits on our freedom, no boundaries to our fun. A few puff clouds dotted the sky. But too soon we felt water at our feet. We broke the dense silence with the irregular rhythm of our rowing and shrieks of distress.

We turned the sinking boat back towards shore. The boat responded sluggishly as more water crept on board. The current was now against us. I hadn't yet learned to swim. None of us had time to think, except for me to consider that my mother would kill me if we sank! We made some headway, inching closer to those pilings— those wonderful majestic pilings that a little earlier had seemed so unworthy of notice, those hallowed pilings that now looked like spires touching the heavens! Two boys came walking along the beach. We yelled to them to help us. They made their way out to the piling nearest us, using the few boards that remained for footings.

"Row for all your worth," the taller of the two commanded. We did, our backs straining, our palms burning and hearts pounding.

"Throw us the rope," he yelled. Tom wound the wet rope around the palm of his hand, then pulled it off his fingers and wound the rest of the rope around those strands. He darted his arm back and threw. The boy stretched out his body, holding onto the piling while his friend held him by the waist. He thrust out his arm, caught the rope, and began to pull in the boat while we futilely splashed water out. Finally arriving at the rotting pier, we hopped out and made our way to shore, our adventure sadly over for the day. Though we knew we had been in danger, we enjoyed the excitement—especially now that we stood safely on land.

My brother Tom initiated an annual circus we held in our basement, a dank, packed dirt floor affair. Tom had a bit of the entrepreneurial spirit about him and charged a five-cent admission to the neighboring kids who attended. I no longer remember if we made flyers to publicize the date and time of the event or if we relied on word of mouth to get the information out, but we always had enough kids to make the circus worthwhile. We decorated the basement with crepe paper streamers and lugged in various folding chairs and boxes for seating. We hung blankets on either side of a central 'stage' so that we could stand in the 'wings' between our acts. I don't remember what my act was, but the highlight of the circus was my brother's performance of the song "You gotta accentuate the positive, eliminate the negative, latch on to the affirmative, don't mess with Mr. In-between," which he sang with crossed eyes while doing a cross-step and twirling a cane.

One summer we learned about a little curly red-haired girl—the daughter, we heard, of the artichoke king—who was studying tap dancing and singing. My brother thought she'd make a great addition and he auditioned her. She was delighted to have a venue to perform in and didn't ask for any 'pay,' but I was against her joining our circus. I was jealous of this little red headed Shirley Temple. She was cute and talented, but Tom prevailed over my weak objections: how could I make a case against having a talented performer included in the show? She attended the rehearsals my brother called, acting like a real trouper, and she did indeed add to our circus that year.

Perhaps my love of dress-up dated to these fly-by-night circus performances. Or maybe it was just part of being a little girl. Around this time, due to the popularity of a dwarf in the Ringling Brothers Barnum and Bailey Circus named Tom Thumb, who had married another dwarf, 'Tom Thumb weddings' were performed in schools across America. I was attending Our Lady of Mercy School on

Washington Square South (where the New York University Law School is now situated). The nuns at the school chose me to be the bride, complete with white gown and veil. Fellow first grader, Georgie—whom we constantly tortured with our sing-song rhyme of "Georgie Porgie, pudding and pie, kissed the girls and made them cry"—was the groom and my dour classmate Stefanie, a bridesmaid. Though I remember this reenactment not at all, I have a photo taken of the 'wedding party.' We're all smiling—Georgie and even dour Stephanie, laughing. I'm surprised by my total lack of memory of the 'wedding,' an event I would have thought unforgettable to a little girl.

But one dress-up I vividly remember was the 'nun' costume. I was in second grade and was to dress in the habit of the French nuns who taught us at Our Lady of Mercy School. Little girls from all over the city dressed in the habit of the nuns who taught them and processed at St. Patrick's Cathedral during Benediction. 'My' nuns had a nifty habit: it had a white pleated fan-like starched wimple. Attached to it was a flowing black veil. I wore a white starched half-moon bib over the bodice and a one-piece, black belted dress with a full skirt.

My mother dressed me in a little room somewhere in St. Patrick's. She braided my hair and pinned the braids at the nape of my neck, so that the veil would fall properly. The headdress made my thin face look fuller. To my delight, my mother put a little lipstick on me. This surprised me since nuns didn't wear lipstick, but I was pleased with the whole ritual—the lipstick, the long voluminous skirt, the white headdress, the black veil. Each little 'nun' was given a straw basket filled with dried roses for scattering as we walked in procession around the cathedral.

The organ rolled and the procession began. I lowered my eyes towards the basket of dried roses. There weren't a great many petals and buds, so—a bit nervous from being in such a large church with all eyes on us little 'nuns'—I assiduously scattered the petals a few at a time as the choir sang and an array of priests prayed at the altar. Incense filled the air. As I was breaking up one of the dried buds into petals when I was half way down the long aisle, a woman, sitting at the end of a pew, reached into my basket and grabbed one of the buds. "You don't mind," she said as she plucked it from my basket.

I *did* mind, but I could do nothing because we were in procession and I had to keep walking. And now I didn't have enough petals to scatter. This upset me very much—so much so that I remember nothing else of the event after that incident.

A formal 8 X 11 inch photo records another dress-up occasion—this one for our eighth grade Christmas play. Each year Sister Ellen had to devise a Christmas pageant that told the same story, but in a different way. This year we were to show a Mexican Christmas with a piñata that we were to bang at the end of the presentation so that the gifts hidden within the papier mâché donkey could spill out onto the stage. This was well before what became children's ubiquitous piñata birthday parties. All of us eighteen students look frozen in our costumes. Nini wears a sarapi, Josephine a Mexican peasant blouse, Tonia a skirt held up by a string looped through a waistband, Geraldine in a similar costume in a different color. All the colors are bright reds, yellows and orange. The photo shows us all round cheeked, not smiling, quite serious due to the religious significance of the event being presented. What the photo doesn't show is the denouement: the piñata breaking is a dud. As hard as we try to break it with our sticks, nothing happens. The papier mâché donkey just keeps turning round and round as we batter it harder and harder. The curtain finally comes down. We put aside our sticks and wonder what went wrong.

During the war, saving was a virtue we all engaged in to help in the fight against the enemy, but we saved dimes for a different reason. President Roosevelt had started a "March of Dimes," as he labeled it, to put money into research for the fight against polio, which he had contracted and which struck countless numbers of children.

Around dinnertime late one afternoon, Tom and I heard the front door rattle. Our father was home. As was our wont, we raced to the front door to be the first to greet him so that we could grab the funny pages from his copy of the

World Telegram. This evening my father also had the March of Dimes booklet to fill the slots with the shiny silver coins before sending it on to the research organization.

I surrendered the paper to my brother and sat with my father at the kitchen table while he fed me dimes to slip into the booklet's slots. A dime back then was a good piece of change: it could buy you a cup of coffee or a small cup of ice cream from the Good Humor man who bicycled with his attached refrigerated wagon, ringing his bells around our Long Beach neighborhood. Ten dimes made a dollar, more than the minimum wage.

At that time polio was a dreaded children's disease. Doctors didn't yet know what caused it and no remedy had been discovered against it. Parents thought swimming in pools had something to do with it because the epidemic always emerged in summer.

One very bright, sunny day towards the end of July, my mother and Mrs. Toner, the mother of Tom's friend Pat, had just finished whispering in front of Mrs. Toner's house on Wyoming Avenue. "Mrs. Toner just told me that Pat contracted polio," my mother began as we ambled home down Park Street. People whispered about certain diseases in those days and some words, like cancer, they never even uttered. Certain words had come through the whispering so that I wasn't totally surprised at my mother's statement.

"I'm worried that Tommy will get polio. He was just playing with Pat a week ago," she continued. My eyes widened. I worried about it too. But Tom never did and we didn't see Pat for the rest of the summer since he was involved in intense rehabilitation. He was one of the fortunate ones in that he didn't have to go into an iron lung, a special metal box that the nurses slid your whole body into to help you breathe. Only Pat's left leg was affected. It became thinner and slightly shorter than his right, but that didn't stop him from becoming a lifeguard who could run as fast as any of the other boys.

It was now August in Long Beach. The high sound of the horn that marked noontime hung in the salt air and wafted through our house. We sat in our living room with its dark green walls and yellow chintz sofa. My brother, lying on the floor, hunched over his pencil drawings of bombers and fighter planes shooting down the enemy.

Our radio was a Philco, a standing piece of furniture four feet high with handsome grain markings. News announcer H. V. Kaltenborn's bass voice rumbled out that he was interrupting our program to bring us a special bulletin. My mother and her guest stopped talking. My brother Tom looked over at me. H. V. continued and announced that the war with Japan was over. My mother whispered, "Finally," and then she fell silent, her eyes lowered. An elderly family friend, Mrs. P., a stout, vigorous woman with a son overseas, brushed away tears from her cheeks. She rose up from the sofa, lumbered to her knees and kissed the floor.

For over three and a half years we had supported the rationing of material and food. Since nylon and silk were used to make parachutes, women smeared their legs with tan coloring and used an eyebrow pencil to draw seams up their legs. Our soldiers needed meat and sugar and so we contented ourselves with what we could get with our ration books, though, as for meat, my mother said our neighbor who was a butcher was "good to her." As for sugar, members of my family weren't big eaters or users of sweets: neither of my parents took sugar in their coffee and my mother wasn't much into baking. This was going to change.

Outside, horns honked. Neighbors streamed out of their houses and rushed towards the main street in town.

My brother Tom jumped up and asked my mother if he could join the celebration. "Mom, can I go see?"

"I wanna go too," I called out.

My mother said okay. "But, Tommy, take care of your sister." she added.

We raced up to Beach Street, following the crowd and passing the flower gardens in full bloom with pink roses and blue hydrangeas. Some families had put clamshells on their front yards in the V for Victory pattern. The shells shined bright white in the sun. At Beach Street people lined up in front of the candy store and the red brick restaurant on either side of the street, jostling each other, and laughing and cheering. Cars and a town fire truck, heavy with revelers, moved slowly past the movie theater where on rainy days we watched Jungle Woman serials, past the drug store with its soda fountain and comic books, past the produce store displaying peaches and oranges in crates. In the absence of crepe paper, some teenagers strung a roll of toilet paper from one side of the street to the other. Tom pulled me to the front of the crowd for a better look at the young boys and girls blowing whistles and waving small American flags.

I kept watching the kids with the toilet paper and the fire engine and police car breaking through the roll as they passed. As often as the paper broke, someone stretched it across the street again. Toilet paper in public seemed scandalous to me, yet no adult in the crowd blinked an eye in surprise.

"Hey, wait for me," I yelled as my brother sifted through the crowd to follow the fire engine. I tagged along behind him, humming "God Bless America," which everyone in the exuberant crowd around me was singing. I threw my arms up in the air when we reached the words, "Stand beside her and guide her" and clapped my hands. Abandon and exuberance marked the mood of the crowd; an unfettered sense of life's possibilities hung in the air. No more rationing of gas. We would be able to drive wherever we wanted, whenever we wanted. And my mother and I wouldn't have to wait on line any more to use our ration cards or to buy silk stockings.

When Tom and I returned home, my mother and Mrs. P. were in the kitchen. Mrs. P. was a wonderful cook, a 'natural,' according to my mother and, since we had sugar to spare, I saw her showing my mother how to make wine biscuits.

"See, Margie," she said, "they're simple to make. Just be sure to alternate the wine and the oil." She handed my mother a wooden spoon.

My mother followed Mrs. P.'s directions, stirring the liquids into the flour. Mrs. P. slid the tray into the small gas oven. In a few minutes, the fragrance of sweet dough floated through the house.

"Are they ready yet?" I asked, my impatience growing as quickly as my hunger.

"Soon, soon," she smiled.

Finally, Mrs. P. slipped a spatula under the softly rounded mounds of wine biscuits and glided them onto a white plate. I reached for one.

"Wait till they cool a bit," Mrs. P. warned.

I did a small twirl in our tiny kitchen. I waited. I planted my feet on the floor in front of the tray and blew on one of the biscuits.

Mrs. P. smiled down on me as I took my first bite. I didn't stop chewing until I finished. As I ate, Mrs. P.'s smile became smaller and softer and a filmy mist of tears glistened in her eyes.

"You like the wine biscuits?" she asked quietly. "They're my son's favorite."

I rarely saw Mrs. P. in a reflective mood. As a matter of fact, my most vivid memories of her are in her Greenwich Village apartment with opera music at a very loud volume streaming through her large living room. The room was furnished in the luxurious heavy style of an earlier era with plush overstuffed chairs, heavy drapes, oriental rugs and a fringed scarf hanging over the baby grand piano. Mr. P. sang along with the opera recording in a loud tenor until he and Mrs. P. began arguing at the top of their voices in operatic discord over some trivial matter. Both were large people with large furniture and large voices, who lived on a grand scale. I found it grand to be a part of it.

All through the war we had babied our black Chevrolet, despite its having the shakes in its steering wheel. Our only choice was to hold onto it since all was directed towards making goods for the war effort, not for consumers. America was not a consumer society then; it was a savings society. People saved bits of tin foil, cans and newspapers, collected and recycled for the war effort. Families put any extra money they had into war savings bonds to invest in our country.

One afternoon a year or two after the war ended, my whole family and I were getting ready to leave our apartment to go out in our car. When we arrived downstairs, our black Chevy was nowhere to be seen. My mother, brother and I scanned the street, searching for our car while my father just stood there.

"Someone must have stolen it," he finally announced. He didn't seem terribly concerned. We all gasped. What were we going to do now?

My father took out his car key and said, "I'll just take the first car that this key opens." We were all taken aback and confused by this unorthodox suggestion. It sounded like stealing.

"Daddy, you can't do that," I protested. My father paid me no attention. He hunched down and tried the key in another black car parked nearby. Nothing happened. He moved to the next car, a maroon Pontiac, and jiggled the key in its front door. The door opened.

"OK," he said. "Let's go."

"Daddy," I protested again in alarm. "How can we? It's not our car."

"Oh yes it is," he laughed heartily, hugely satisfied with how well his surprise had gone. "I bought it this afternoon."

Excited, we all hopped in to go for a drive in our brand new car, my father and brother in the front seat and my mother and me in back.

"Ooh, look how steady its steering wheel is," I said as I leaned over the front seat.

"And it has a heater!" my mother exclaimed. "Does it work, Sal?" The 'heater' in our Chevy was a thick gray blanket.

My father turned the new heater on.

"That feels good," my mother announced as the first bit of heated air drifted back to us. "Now we won't have to use the heavy car-blanket any more to stay warm back here," she added.

"What a smooth ride." My brother sighed. "Maybe I won't get car-sick anymore."

"I sure hope not. And look how roomy it is," I added as I stretched out my legs. My father laughed, pleased at our pleasure. We didn't give another thought to our trusty black Chevy. We were on to other things.

After the war there was a pent-up demand for consumer goods. We bought a refrigerator for our summerhouse and Frank converted his ice-truck to a soda truck. He embodied perseverance and dogged determination as he lugged the heavy cases of soda into the various houses. My mother felt a loyalty to Frank since he was just a fellow Italian trying to make a living, but she didn't believe in her children drinking Coke or Pepsi. She solved her dilemma by ordering large bottles of Cream Soda that, at dinner, she allowed us to mix, half and half, with milk. To us it tasted like an ice cream soda.

As a special treat after supper, we occasionally added chocolate syrup and a scoop of ice cream for the 'real thing.' I say occasionally because we rarely had ice cream at home: our new refrigerator didn't have a freezer. All it had was a small compartment in the refrigerator itself holding a few trays of ice cubes. Whenever we bought a half-gallon container of ice cream late in the afternoon, we removed the ice cube trays to make room for the ice cream to be eaten that very night lest it turn into a melted disaster.

Around this time my father told me about a new invention called television—like a radio with a moving picture, he explained. All I could picture was our three-foot tall Philco radio with its flat top having a movie on it that you stood over to watch. Maybe I wasn't so far wrong; one of our neighbors in Long Beach bought a television set very early on. A Motorola, I believe, with a round screen placed flat on a shelf and pointing at the ceiling. The screen reflected onto a mirror, set perpendicular to it at the back of the cabinet for easy viewing. This arrangement had something to do with the large size of the television tube housed below the screen. If the screen with its attached tube had been placed facing its viewers, as it was later, the set would have been four or more feet in depth, too bulky to place against a wall.

Another consumer item my father bought was an eight-millimeter movie camera that produced home movies in color. We could never think of doing much in front of the camera except walk towards it, or swim a few strokes, or stage a running race between Tom and me. Once at Christmas time at my Uncle Louie's house in Riverdale, we all individually walked out the front door in procession—aunts, uncles and cousins, including cousin Louis, who had returned home on furlough. His mother, my Aunt Edna, was busy with the meal, but she stuck her head out the door, waving some stalks of celery. We all laughed when she did that and laughed again when we saw it on film.

Once with my father's camera, I staged a story—a silent movie, of course, since our early cameras had no sound—using my classmates to play the characters—while I wrote, directed and shot the scenes, all done outdoors so that I wouldn't have to deal with the cumbersome lights needed for indoor shootings: four flood lights mounted in a row on a horizontal bar which screwed into the top of the camera. Where that film is or what the story I made up was about, I have no idea, but it satisfied my creative bent.

Our cousins and other relatives and family friends visited us at Long Beach frequently enough so that my mother concocted a solution to the restrictions of our three-bedroom house. She put two mattresses—mattresses were much thinner then than now—on the beds in the two back bedrooms. When guests stayed over, the top mattress was placed on the floor in the dining room and that's where we kids slept while the adults slept in the bedrooms. We loved being allowed to sleep on the floor and fought over being selected to 'go to the mattresses' on those nights when only one bed was needed. We viewed such an arrangement as another sort of freedom associated with Long Beach—namely, misrule, where we kids could whisper late into the night on the floor.

About a half mile from our house, Long Beach had a boardwalk built parallel to the shoreline. The first half of the boardwalk had nothing built up around it. Only sand and ocean on one side and sea grass on the other. No artificial lighting or lampposts were to be seen. Our whole family often walked there on a weekend evening. We'd stroll along for about a mile, hearing the waves lap against the shore and seeing the moon glistening on the water. All was hushed and in shadow, mysterious, yet welcoming and comforting with the moon and stars looking down upon us in that enclosed expansiveness of sea and sky. Though the stars were far away, they seemed familiar to us in that protective world.

After about a mile, the boardwalk changed from its naturally beautiful surroundings to a kids' wonderland with a bit of honky tonk thrown in. There were rides—the whip, a Ferris wheel, bumper cars, small boats that moved in a stationary circle, food stands for hot dogs, cotton candy, and ice cream, and a penny arcade for us to enjoy.

When we arrived at the rides, my mother always asked, "Going on the Whip as usual?" It was my favorite—separate cars that whirled round and round, faster and faster, causing me to delight in my stomach's lurchings on the whipping motions. After that we ordered ice cream cones. I liked tutti frutti as much for its name as its flavor. And finally we reached the penny arcade. The glass encased 'gypsy lady' statue, wearing a black lace shawl and red turban, stood at the front of the arcade. As I pushed my penny into the slot, the gypsy moved from side to side, eyes opening and closing, arms bent at the elbow, palms down hovering over playing cards, until a fortune card dropped into a slot. I'd live to be eighty-four, the card said.

I played a skills game of a car's wheel that I steered on a moving road displayed on a screen behind it—so simple compared to the video games of today. My brother liked other kinds of games, such as pinball with flashing lights. We ate cotton candy, unconcerned that its gooey sweetness was traced on our faces. With mincing steps, elderly women, out to see and be seen, teetering on high heels and wearing mink stoles, avoided our sticky hands and smeared faces.

My father was what my mother called a "sport." If I invited a friend to join us, he would treat her to all that the boardwalk had to offer. I didn't think of that as unusual, but the father of my friend Susan was not like that. He would never treat. I had the feeling that they were on a strict budget. Susan's mother worked at home, drawing clothing advertisements for newspapers. Though I recognized Mrs. K.'s talent, it never occurred to me then that she might actually have chosen to work. This was at a time when few women worked outside the home. Poorer women, like my aunt and godmother, and grandmother before them, had always worked, usually in factories for Italian women—perhaps, as Gambino writes in *Blood of*

My Blood, due to the injunction against Italian women cleaning houses where they could come in contact with men. If we take Mozart's *Marriage of Figaro* seriously, unmarried women certainly had cause to avoid the situation of the right of the *padrone,* in whose home they worked, to sleep with them on the night before their wedding.

Mrs. K. and her husband did serious fishing—to stretch their food budget, by my lights—and made me think they had to watch their pennies.

One day while I was there, Mr. K. a came flying through the front door. "Hey, honey," he called to his wife who was drawing at her worktable in the living room. "Sam says the fish are biting." Mrs. K. laid her pencil at the side of her drawing paper. They rushed to the back porch, grabbed their fishing poles and ran towards the bay.

Another day they caught a lobster among the rocks at the ocean. When they arrived home, they put it in a pot. Susan started to set the table.

"Yikes," she yelled. "The lobster got out. Over there. It's scurrying along the floor." Susan pointed towards the table as we ran this way and that, not wanting the lobster to nip us. Mrs. K. scooped it up with one hand—the lobster's claws were waving wildly—filled the pot with water, plunked it into the pot again, clapped on a lid and, while holding it down, turned on the gas flame. The lobster made scratching noises for as long as it was able against its entrapment, before quieting down.

Other neighbors of ours had one daughter who was about three or four years older than I. Despite the age difference, we played street games and board games together and when she learned to drive, Jean Anne asked me to accompany her and her friend Arlene on a drive. Jean Anne was already a fussy spinster type—she never did marry—who spoke in a nasal whiny voice and had an inordinate fear of insects. While driving along, a fly got in the car and Jean Anne panicked causing us to bump lightly—we were already slowing down for a stop sign— into the car in front of us. No damage was done to either car and we were quickly on our way again.

"Promise you won't tell my mother," Jean Anne commanded fearfully.

Arlene and I promised since we didn't want any future expeditions cancelled. I remember no other car rides after that, but I do remember a bike ride we three took into Rockville Center, nine miles away. Except for Long Beach Road, a well-traveled thoroughfare, we stuck to back roads for our bike trip. Arlene and Jean Anne had trim three-speed bikes with slim tires while mine was an old clunker with old-fashioned fat tires and no speed changes. We were riding to Rockville Center to visit a friend of Jean Anne's who had won some beauty contest— perhaps it was a beauty contest that the town held. Beauty contests were popular in those days with Miss America being every young girl's idol.

It took us a long time to reach her friend's house and I

was impressed with not only how pretty her friend was, but how unlike Jean Anne she was—not fussy, but just a regular, and sweet, young woman. After about an hour of chatting, we left to make our way back home. It was now the middle of the afternoon and the sun was beating down on us. I struggled along on my bike, switching between standing up to get some momentum going and sitting down to coast while Jean Anne and Arlene waited for me. At one point, we got off our bikes to rest for a moment.

"Carol," Jean Anne screamed. "Your dungarees are ripped."

I quickly tried to look behind me to see how extensive the rip was, but I couldn't get the proper angle. I felt around the back of my pants for the rip. It wasn't small. I must have caught my pants on a scratchy part of the seat as I alternated between standing and sitting on the bike. I immediately hopped back up on my bike and we continued on our trek home. My trusty bike and I were none the worse for wear, ready for our next adventure.

The summer before I entered eighth grade, Sister Ellen gave our class a list of books we had to read over the vacation before entering her class. When we got out of school for the summer, I dutifully started going through the list, reading on rainy days in Long Beach when we couldn't go to the beach. The book I most remember reading was Booker T. Washington's memoir *Up from Slavery*. The specifics of the deprived life of the former slaves as they entered Tuskegee impressed me. To this day I still remember Washington's descriptions of blacks that didn't own a toothbrush or had never slept in a bed with sheets and blankets.

My father saw the book lying around and he too read it and found it as compelling as I had. My interest in the book was partly due to the fact that, though my family gave few particulars about their parents' lives in Italy, or their work lives in America, or about their *own* impoverished childhoods, I intuited that, in the way my grandparents had been treated, they were really just one step above the slaves.

My mother and her women friends enjoyed telling stories about how the Italian women had their babies right in the field in which they were toiling and then immediately went back to work. Although these stories were always told with pride and awe at the strength of our ancestors, whose own children could not live up to their mothers' heroics, for me the feeling lingered that my grandmother's generation had led lives very similar to slaves.

Reinforcing that thought that autumn, our studies in school included a unit on child labor laws. Our eighth-grade history book showed an illustration of a little girl, crawling on her hands and knees in a mine. Why it showed a young *girl* in a mine has puzzled me to this day since I've never read that any girls went into the mines. Most probably I've misremembered it. Be that as it may, I also don't know if the line drawing in black and white was a cartoon from the era urging protection of child laborers or if it was a recent drawing to depict how children's lives had been. In any case, that drawing terrified me. It could have been my mother, I thought to myself, who was working in America during that era.

So compelling was that image in the mine that it made me want to enter a mine to see for myself what it was like for the workers. Years later, when I was well over fifty, on a hot and humid June day, my husband and I were visiting Scranton, Pennsylvania to see the lovely public library his grandfather had built for the city modeled after a building in Paris, France. This was coal country. My husband's grandfather had made his money by selling anthracite.

A closed mine in the area had been turned into an educational tour. I was eager to enter the mine. While we waited for our turn to be carried down into the bottom of the mine, I perused the exhibition of original photos of miners at work along with explanatory information. I read that boys as young as six years old worked in the mines. The guides now employed here were either ex-miners or the descendents of miners, some of whom had gone on to receive Ph.D.s in history.

My husband and I entered the train, sitting in the first seat, which was to carry us into the mine ten stories below. Affixed to the front car was the original sign in six different languages warning riders to keep their arms within the open-sided car. The car creaked and groaned along the rails as we blundered deeper and deeper into the bowels of the mine. The atmosphere was steadily getting danker, colder and darker. We got out of the car. The guide warned us to avoid the water that dripped constantly along the walls and pooled on the lumpy floor. Small lights—not installed when the mine was worked—illuminated the gloom somewhat for us tourists so we could see the mock-ups of miners at work: the brake-boy, a mule and cart, etc.

As the guide talked about various aspects of mining, all I could think about was getting out. This was a hell no better than the one Dante described. Hadn't there ever been a sensitive six-year-old who refused to go back down into the mine after one day of torment? Upon emerging from the tunnels—so dark that even with an occasional light for us tourists, we could barely see in front of us—I asked our guide, an ex-miner, about children working down there. His response was that when people come from countries where they're starving, as the miners did, they have no alternative but to be a miner, a fairly well paying job, despite the danger, for a worker with no skills. That ended the discussion, but I thought about two of my father's cousins who had immigrated to America with my grandfather and had worked in the coalmines of Pennsylvania. My grandfather never heard from them again.

My father was twenty years younger than his youngest brother. The two oldest brothers had both served in World War I, but my father didn't have to worry about being called up for military service during the Second World War, because he was too old to serve. He was no doubt grateful for that since he was busy working and putting his small family on a sound financial footing—something that he had not known as a child. He was the son of a poor immigrant (from Anzi in Basilicata, Italy) who was hard-pressed just to put enough food on the table every night. His town was near Aliano, which Carlo Levi made famous in his book, *Christ Stopped at Eboli*. Set in the nineteen thirties, Levi had been 'exiled' there from his northern hometown because he was an anti-fascist. The work, which was also made into a movie with the wonderful Greek actress, Irene Pappas, is a poignant account of the people of the town and their customs, unchanged for eons, and demonstrates the political corruption that was endemic to so much of southern Italy. Its portrayal of the mayor suggests the vested interest of so many in keeping the peasants ignorant; the portrayal of the priest surely explains the anti-clericalism of some Italians.

My maternal grandmother was born in Lauropoli, Calabria and died at the age of a hundred and one in the nineteen seventies. When I was a teenager, she—not a literate woman—told me a mélange of two Greek myths (which unfortunately I no longer recall). Her town was part of Magna Grecia so I can only conclude that these stories had passed down through two millennia via the oral tradition.

She had at least three sisters I know of. She was very close to her youngest sister, Anna Maria, who was twenty years younger than she. When her sister was born, their mother was sick so that my grandmother, who was nursing her own son, also nursed her sister. This accounts for their closeness.

Around 1976 on one of my many trips to Italy, I visited my grandmother's siblings who had remained in Lauropoli. Anna Maria was about seventy-six at the time. She had had a difficult life. She had been widowed young, her only son had been killed in the Second World War, and she had six daughters. They had struggled to survive farming their bit of land. During the war my grandmother collected clothing from all our neighbors and regularly mailed them a large package of used clothing to use or possibly to sell or exchange the surplus for other supplies.

When I arrived at Lauropoli, I found Anna Maria sitting in front of her home—a one-story, little white concrete box of a house. Many in the town had moved from the old town into this new section. Anna Maria sat outside on a straight-backed chair, surrounded by her daughters and one granddaughter. Her daughters' husbands had migrated to Germany to work as electricians. Her front door was open, but I could see nothing of the interior that, partly due to the bright sunlight blinding me, looked like a dark, deep space. She was an extremely thin woman—

and she was blind. I was not expecting this because my grandmother had sent Anna Maria money to have a cataract operation. But as we chatted in her dialect, it became clear to me that she was a product of the culture of poverty: like many Italian peasants, she didn't trust doctors or hospitals. She believed that those who entered a hospital died there because, like the poor the world over, that had been their experience of receiving the worst health care.

Before I left for Italy, my grandmother had given me one hundred twenty-five dollars to hand over personally to Anna Maria. After I exchanged the dollars into lire—it came to about two hundred thousand lire at the time—I handed the thick wad of money to her. She took it, rolled it tightly, and stuck it between her flattened breasts, a gesture I had occasionally seen practiced in my own neighborhood.

My grandmother's other living sister, Concetta, had had a very different sort of life. She was about eighty-six at the time I met her. She looked like a slightly younger version of my grandmother who was then ninety-six. Concetta lived with her son and his family in a lovely, modernized apartment overlooking the main plaza. Not only did she look like my grandmother, but she also had the same personality—sprightly, outgoing, humorous, and, I suspected as I observed her behavior with her son and daughter-in-law, domineering her children as my grandmother had domineered my mother.

On my return, my mother told me that Concetta's husband had worked in America for ten years and that upon his return to Italy the money he had saved during those years abroad had been instrumental in their bettered standard of living.

My grandmother had at least one brother, Luigi, who lived in Memphis, not a section of America where many Italian immigrants lived. When the railroad he was working on ended construction in Tennessee, he stayed in the area. He and my grandmother only saw each other once when she went by train with her daughter Rose and Rose's daughter Lillie to visit him and his family.

My godmother Lillie recounted a story that demonstrates the differences between the southern and northern branches of the family. The Tennessee branch would sit out on their porch and when it was announced that the spaghetti was ready, they would continue sitting on the porch chatting. This tardiness to dinner would never have happened up North.

The Southerners also ate less than their New York relatives so that one night while visiting there Lillie, by no means a prodigious eater, was reduced to lining up eight pistachios on the mantel in her room, spacing out the eating of them to ease her hunger.

A few years later, two women, Luigi's granddaughters, I believe— one was a lawyer by the name of Mary Guida—came to visit us in New York City. We all enjoyed hearing these women speak Italian with my grandmother in a southern American drawl.

Molly Goldberg was one of our neighbors in Long Beach. She was Irish Catholic. She had married a Jewish man, named Dan. They had a son Stewart who was a year or two older than I. Steward was sweet on me but unfortunately I liked his mother better.

A competent woman, she was one of the few mothers I knew who worked outside the home. A husky woman with a husky voice from years of nonstop smoking, she dominated her household even though she was gone during the day. She was easy going, organized and relaxed. She always had something interesting to say and had the facility to talk easily with anyone. Although she was an adult, she could speak to us teenagers without condescension and yet maintain her adult standing.

During the winter, Mrs. Goldberg would invite me down to Long Beach to stay with her family when my summer choir gave its winter concert of Handel's *Messiah*. The Goldbergs had two homes in Long Beach, one in the East End, which was their winter home and which they rented in the summer, and another in the West End on our block for summer living. So I'd stay with the family in the East End and also visit with my best friend Liz who by that time was living in the West End of Long Beach year round with her family. Liz was a tall, chubby, pigeon-toed redhead with an infectious laugh who looked for things to laugh about. And she had a crush on Stewie. The device to put me more in contact with him actually worked to forward a romance between the two of them.

I enjoyed my visits with Mrs. Goldberg immensely. For years afterwards, I maintained a correspondence with her. And no, Liz and Stew never married. He married another Long Beach neighbor who lived right behind us.

A few years after my father died, my mother sold our summerhouse. Long Beach eventually gentrified, becoming home for people working in the city, offering as it did an easy commute, easy living and I hope as many happy memories as it held for me. My generation had realized one aspect of the promise of America.

Chapter 5

Springtime Stumblings

Our neighbor Millie had come by to thank my grandmother for curing her daughter's fever by praying over her barrettes.

I didn't look directly at Millie's body, fearing that I'd seem too curious about her stomach, big as a watermelon, hiking up the hem of her housedress. I wanted to touch that fat round ball, feel its fullness and know its secrets.

I watched my mother accompany Millie down our entry hall. As she opened the front door, I could see another neighbor, Angela, gliding by. A stunning blonde, who wore her hair in a sophisticated chignon, which set off her high cheekbones and white teeth, Angela was a model. Her elegant movements had an unaffected grace. Always dressed in an understated way in the latest fashions, she wore well-tailored suits, subdued colors, and shoes with matching handbags.

Once the war was over, Angela switched from wearing the short straight skirts and three-quarter length coats that cloth rationing demanded to wearing the New Look: ruffled blouses, gored skirts, full coats that rippled with excess cloth at the back and platform shoes. No longer did she carry crocheted handbags, but rather ones made of buttery leather.

To us kids her beauty separated her from us. She existed on some higher, rarefied level. We never felt sufficiently worthy to greet her. Silenced by her beauty, we admired her from a distance. I had never heard her say a word. She adored Frank Sinatra and had found and married a young man from the neighborhood who was Sinatra's double. Angela nodded to Millie and my mother, but she didn't stop to chat.

The next day I was strolling down Sixth Avenue from Greenwich House, where I went for after-school programs. I was focusing on modern dance with Miss Lipton. We had just practiced a dance I choreographed. We girls—Gina, Kathy, Gloria and I—played hunters, stalking a tiger. Our teacher, Miss Lipton, a short young woman with fine light hair, came every Monday after school to give us a dance class. She was part of the bohemian world that made up the non-Italian half of Greenwich Village: she wore her hair in a long pony-tail and changed right in front of us in the locker room, not turning her back as she slipped on a fresh bra. But we girls, having been trained by nuns even if we attended different schools, turned our backs modestly away from each other when we changed in the locker room. In Miss Lipton's case, we weren't so modest as not to look at her and compare our bodies to hers. We were fumbling our way towards adulthood.

As I ambled along Sixth, I spied Angela the model from our apartment building, looking as beautiful as ever. Her black high heels didn't interfere with her graceful walk and erect posture. She had a dynamism that suggested a calm purposefulness. Men turned to look at her. I stared after her too, her tall, willowy body unhurried by the congestion along the avenue. She strode past the Waverly movie house. I crossed the street and stopped to look at the movie posters.

When I went to the movies I felt a total immersion in the stories up on the screen. On seeing *Heidi*, I emerged from the movie house with my tear-streaked face; at the film *Pinocchio*, an usher asked me to leave due to my loud sobbing. I lived those days in the magic of storytelling. In my seat in the darkened theater, I was so caught up in the movie's story that I unconsciously mouthed the actors' words and mimicked their facial expressions. Rita Hayworth's beauty in *Gilda* left me breathless.

Four months earlier, I had totally succumbed to theater. In November I had attended my first Broadway play, *Peter Pan* with Mary Martin, and, tears welling in my eyes, I had clapped furiously so that Tinker Bell would not die. I believed in magic just as my mother and Millie believed in my grandmother's magical prayers murmured over an object casting a spell. I would have been horrified if some of my classmates had seen me clapping for Tinker

Bell. Such enchantment at my age was something none of us wanted to be accused of. We were trying to become adults.

A few blocks downtown on Sullivan Street, opposite St. Anthony's Church, I bought a Charlotte Russe, which was sitting in the little glass stand outside the candy store. Thick paper wound around the white cake with a mountain of whipped cream on top. Peeling away the paper a little at a time, I could eat the cake and cream together. I tore a bit of the paper away, pushed my mouth greedily against the cream, and took a large bite. The cream squeezed out the sides of my mouth. I licked the escaping cream with my tongue and finished off the Charlotte Russe.

The next day, a Wednesday, Sister Ellen Mary, our eighth grade teacher at St. Joseph Academy, sent Mike, tall and good-looking—a leader among the boys—and me on separate errands to other teachers. As we were returning to our classroom, he and I bumped into each other on the stairs. Mike, his straight black hair slicked back and his dark eyes bright, chucked me under the chin and said, "That's not all I'll do to you next time." His words and the touch of his fingers, lingering under my chin and brushing my neck, excited me. What *would* he do? Would he take me in his arms? Would he kiss me?

It wouldn't be my first kiss. That had occurred the past summer at our beach house. It had been a long kiss, so long in fact that it had taken my breath away—not because of the ardor I felt, but because I had been swimming that day and my sinuses were acting up. I could only breathe through my mouth, and since the boy's mouth covered my lips, I was left breathless. Concentrating on not bursting for want of air, I couldn't fully respond to his soft lips pressed against mine as his arm gently pulled me close. My stuffy sinuses had smothered my first real kiss, but not so much that I hadn't enjoyed it and understood the delights of two bodies close together, lips moving and responding to each other in an elaborate dance. Now, I was almost a year older and my hormones, if not raging, were well into play; I daily waited for, and longed for, Mike's next move.

A year younger than my classmates, I at times grew bored with some of the girls whose only interest was boys. While I certainly liked boys, or at least some of them—I had a new crush every other week—the interest of some of the girls seemed obsessive: some were planning a formal dance for graduation with all of us girls to wear evening gowns. It seemed like overkill, but I was game.

Later in the school day at recess, Faye, Gerry, and Barbara huddled together in a tight circle, making plans. "We'll wear gowns and the boys will wear their blue suits," Barbara said.

"Yeah, and we'll bring records for dancing," Faye added.

To my disappointment, my mother offered to hobble together a limp gown, no longer in style, from Millie's teenage years of long ago when her stomach was flat. My mother's frugal ways made me pass on the dance.

My school was housed in a five-story red brick building with a long, graceful white staircase—wider at the bottom with softly curving banisters at either side—that we students were rarely allowed to use. We entered on the ground floor at the door below, painted black and always in shadow, hidden beneath the stoop. In its time this darkened area had been the servants' entrance. Having been converted from a very comfortable home overlooking Washington Square Park, the building still retained signs of gracious living: a large oriental rug in the auditorium, marble mantelpieces flanked by tall, standing Oriental vases, paintings and etchings on the walls. But we students lined up by class in the gym on the floor below, where we also ate lunch every day and had ballroom dance lessons on Fridays with Miss Ingaborg Torib. She also coached our dramatic productions and was said to have been an actress. Her husky voice gave no nonsense directions in both dancing class and at play rehearsals.

Miss Torib, a svelte, willowy woman with a fuzz of white hair, wore long flowing black skirts and a leotard top—all very form fitting. She was both long-waisted and long-legged, which added to her grace as she stretched out her long narrow feet sinuously in front of her. She taught us the foxtrot, waltz, and tango with a folk dance or two thrown in. Protected by white gloves that both the boys and girls were required to wear, we executed the steps stiffly as if we were following instructions to solve a math problem. The boys wore navy blue suits with white shirts and dark ties. We girls wore maroon jumpers with straight skirts and belts that tied us up like sacks. Dance shoes— little black Capezio ballerinas—did little to lighten our steps or to protect us from the boys' stumblings in their brown oxfords. We counted out the tango steps: one, two, step-touch-side-together in rhythm, with us quickly chanting the last four words. We went through the motions of this most amorous dance woodenly while Miss Torib glided inside the circle of dancing couples, her shiny skirt dancing at the hem from the thrust of her legs as they snaked forward. In her cigarette voice, she prompted us girls to "tighten your buttocks and tuck them in," hers rising and falling as she demonstrated—now tight and tucked, now relaxed. Clinging material sheathed Miss Torib's tall slender body, her white hair crowned her head. She held her chin high. She threw back her shoulders, thrust her small bosom forward, and controlled her buttocks while her delicate white ankles sneaked forward from under her long skirt.

By way of contrast, the nuns stood with their black bonnets (and man's length hair hidden beneath), black capes falling from shoulder to waist and voluminous skirts from which their black oxfords peeked—assuring us that legs did indeed exist beneath the multiple layers of cloth. The nuns never referred to any body parts, yet they accepted this woman, clearly not from a world of theirs or ours with her directions on how to hold our bodies and how adult women should carry themselves. On Monday I danced in Miss Lipton's class and on Friday in Miss Torib's. Unwittingly the presence and carriage of these two women created alternative worlds of womanhood to the nuns.

The nuns were tolerant of artists and the various non-Catholic women who gave us special classes in singing, speech, and drawing. Their tolerance seemed to stem from an acceptance of other life styles. It was impossible to avoid such differences in Greenwich Village—and although neither they nor any of us were ever expected to imitate such lifestyles (heaven forbid!), the nuns seemed willing to co-exist with such adults and to expose us to their unique talents. In their dedication to getting Catholics into the mainstream of American life, the nuns were pragmatic about making use of whatever they thought would help affect this result.

If David Brooks of *The New York Times* is any judge, as a group Catholic immigrants lived up to and even surpassed the ambitions the nuns had for us, if not quite in the way the nuns would have wished. In a 2007 article in that newspaper, Brooks writes about an "economic boom among quasi-religious Catholics." And that's the rub as far as the nuns would be concerned. As we Catholics of immigrant ancestors came to adulthood, our links to the church weakened and we assimilated. We became more individualistic, more future oriented, according to Brooks, and we are much better educated than our family histories would have predicted. These traits, coupled with high marriage rates and low divorce rates as well as being big savers and favoring low-risk investments, Brooks writes, are responsible for our success as a group. He concludes, "...the children of white, ethnic, blue-collar neighborhoods have managed to adapt the Catholic communal heritage to the dynamism of a global economy."

The Federal Census of 2000 confirms these findings for Italian Americans. Compared to the general population, Italian Americans have the highest percentage of positions in managerial and professional occupations and they have the highest percentage of physicians and surgeons and lawyers. Compared to the general population again, Italian Americans have the highest family median income.

The nuns were Irish Americans. They told us about "No Irish need apply" signs and how at one time Catholics in public schools had to listen to readings from the Protestant Bible. They resented the fact that Protestants had discriminated against Catholics and excluded them from certain schools, positions and organizations. We were to be the generation of Catholics who would break down any remaining barriers in education and employment and bring our Catholic values to the places that had excluded us in the past. The nuns expected great things of us and inspired our ambitions.

From Miss Torib we would learn another way of being an adult. She was from that world which we knew about only from glimpses: the artists wearing berets on Carmine Street, the dancers walking along in their legwarmers on Barrow, the photographers in their studios with highly stylized portraits displayed in sedate windows along Jones Street. But we students discovered nothing about Miss Torib—no overheard comments, no dropped information to glean how the other half, the bohemians, *really* lived behind closed doors. Though I considered her old, her allure was obvious: I pictured her in her apartment languidly standing by a baby grand piano in one of her flowing outfits, cigarette in hand, surrounded by a coterie of male admirers.

One afternoon after school, Sister Ellen invited me into her adult world by reading me a children's version of *The Tempest* she had written for possible use for our graduation play. She sat at her desk with papers spread out in front of her, reading from her manuscript. When she used the word 'seduced,' I interrupted.

"What does 'seduced' mean?"

"Oh, uh..." She swiped at some loose hair that had escaped from her bonnet and tucked it out of sight again into her cap. Sitting back in her chair, she slid the notebook towards the middle of her desk and shut it, her white hands splayed flat on its cover.

"It...it means kidnapped," she stuttered at last.

I barely breathed, willing my face into a bland

expression as if I were unaware of Sister's embarrassed stammerings. I registered her nervous evasion silently while not betraying my own interest in and musings on the reason for her duplicity. Her evident discomfort with my asking what the word meant made me look it up in our fat two-volume dictionary as soon as I arrived home.

I wasn't totally surprised that Sister Ellen would hedge about the definition. Sexuality wasn't something nuns, especially Irish-American nuns, were comfortable talking about, but I was disappointed in her because she had seemed more open and progressive than most of the other nuns. Perhaps I had been misled by the fact that she was the only nun I had ever known whose curves could be seen through her habit, making her seem like a sexual creature.

As usual my mother was waiting for me on the park bench chatting with some of the students' mothers. I strolled over to her, said hello to my classmate Junior's much older sister, and stood and watched the boys for a minute as they played stickball against the Arch. Junior's petite sister was very pretty but she wore pancake make-up—a very thick make-up that preceded the lighter liquid ones. My mother questioned her about it. "Such a pretty girl like you doesn't need all that thick goop on her face." I secretly agreed.

My mother and I wended our way home, waving to Mr. Cardinale, who was sitting in front of his flower store across the street. He sat backwards in his wooden chair, his hands dangling listlessly over the back, watching two boys racing by in their orange-crate wagons with roller-skate wheels. We passed the neighborhood photographer's store, with his photos of fighters like Rocky Marciano next to those of neighborhood girls in white wearing First Holy Communion veils. In the window as well, the storeowner had displayed the bridal photo of Angela the model from our apartment house with her groom, the Frank Sinatra look-alike.

We entered the hardware store that sold *lupini—chi-chi* beans in dialect—soaking in salt water. We bought some that I munched as we walked along, stopping at Zito's Bakery for some hardtack bread, a favorite of my grandmother's and mine.

I was surprised to see Angela waiting in line at the bakery. Perfectly coiffed, she was as glowing in person as she was in her bridal photo. My mother and she made small talk while we waited to be served.

"How's your mother, Angela?" my mother asked

"Oh, she's awright...you know."

"Such a sweet woman," my mother added.

"Yeah...so, I mean...what's new with you?" Angela asked.

My mouth fell open. I had never heard her speak. She was dumb. Her raw, coarse voice contained no sense of graciousness to match her beauty. She was beautiful, yes, but so stupid she couldn't even carry on small talk.

When we left the bakery, my mother drove home the

point. "You can know what someone is like from the moment they 'open their mouth,'" she said. Such knowledge was big in my neighborhood. If you spoke with an accent, you were a 'greenhorn.' If you said 'youse,' you were, through no fault of your own, uneducated. If your voice was raw and unmodulated, you had no aspirations. If you used big words, you could be seen as trying to lord it over others.

In the fall of 1951 things changed. I went off to high school, located on the Upper East Side with its apartment buildings and private schools scattered about it, and St. Ignatius Loyola Church dominating the corner of 84th and Park Avenue. No food markets lined the broad avenues— not even a D'Agostino's—so unlike my neighborhood with the warm aroma of its coffee bean shop, the slightly vinegary smell of the cheese store and the pungent odor of the pork butcher's. On the Upper East Side you'd see Don Ameche, every inch the gentleman in his camel's hair coat, strolling on Madison Avenue, ambling along as if he hadn't a care in the world.

Other changes in circumstances occurred. In our building Angela the model, divorced now, was involved in a paternity suit. It was in all the papers, which described her as a high-priced call girl. I tried to make sense of such goings on. If the nuns had seen Angela as she walked by school, I doubt that they would have guessed at her unsavory background. She looked so wholesome in her beauty with her clean-scrubbed look. Her appearance kept secret her voice, its coarseness not revealed.

I started going to the dances at the Jesuit boys' high school across the street from St. Lawrence Academy. Mike, my chin-chucking classmate from eighth grade, was at one of the dances. Much to my disappointment, he had never followed through with his braggadocio posturing of the year before, but that night when he asked me to dance, he pulled me close and held me tight in his arms—no room for the Holy Ghost, as the saying went in Catholic high schools. We danced together for the rest of the night, I dreamily thinking he was wonderful, all thoughts of nuns' interdictions far from my mind as I snuggled against Mike's wool jacket. I couldn't wait to see him again—and I didn't have to wait long. We met again at The James, a Madison Avenue diner, owned by a German couple with heavy accents, where we high school students hung out. I often wrote doggerel poetry—not all of it kind— about the students attending dances, basketball games, and other student activities. I would either read them or pass them around at the James. Mike and I sat in a booth with some of the other students and talked after we passed around my poems.

But I was perplexed. I didn't find him exciting as I had at the dance and I couldn't figure out why. Confused, I didn't know what it was that I saw in him that night.

Meanwhile, Angela won her paternity case and married a rich playboy. But her bridal photo with her Sinatra look-alike groom remained in the photographer's window. The charm of the photo and her beauty couldn't be denied. She moved out of our neighborhood and we neither saw her again nor read about her in the papers.

One rainy day Sue, who had attended grammar school with me and now, high school, and I slurped ice cream sodas at the soda fountain in the pharmacy on West 10th Street. Sue was tall with deep-set brooding eyes. I often saw her sulking in class even though when we were together, she laughed a lot—or more accurately—giggled. By dint of her sense of her own maturity as well as her greater physical development, Sue was the leader of a small group of us girls, Judy, Tonia, Sheila, and me. She was not only much more developed than the rest of us— she wore tight tee-shirts which showed off her ample, almost matronly, bosom—but she was also an odd combination of willed innocence and worldly knowledge and seemed to deny the fact that she was growing up. She still wore her blond hair in braids—although sometimes she gave herself a more adult look by pinning her braids at the nape of her neck. But then she'd switch to wearing them in circles at the side of her head—a little Dutch-girl look. She didn't use deodorant when she obviously needed to. And yet she had a great interest in all the details of adult sexuality.

Her father was a sea captain and away a lot. Maybe that was the reason she spent her summers with her grandmother on a farm in Maryland. She spoke in great detail about her encounters with one of the young black workers on the farm. She had a Southern attitude towards him, treating him in a condescending way one minute—laughing about how stupid he was—and in the next minute telling me what fun the two of them had had riding together in a wagon.

"Jessie and I were doing the haying together," she began. "It was fun having someone else to do it with. I was really sweaty. Jessie was too and, boy, did he stink. He needs to wash more. I threw hay at him to cover the smell," she giggled. "And I pushed him away from me. He stumbled and fell so I threw more hay on him, rubbing it down his neck and onto his chest. We were both laughing... I was practically rolling on top of him. Anyway, we rode back in the wagon towards the farm. We had to sit real close, 'cause there wasn't much space up front. He turned towards me...I was kind of leaning towards him...I don't know what he was thinking! Such a jerk."

She *wanted* him to kiss her! And she couldn't admit it—not even to herself. Her desire maybe even confused her—or frightened her a little and left her feeling angry. For all of her seeming maturity, she was as confused as any of us. I mumbled something or other when she was done speaking. And then I found myself telling her about Mike and the 'chuck' under the chin and his bravado. She gazed at me from under her bleached lashes, then glanced away, but in that gaze I saw something—not jealousy, no, not that. Worse than that—longing, a terrible yearning and I understood that feeling.

I began to realize that people could be attracted to each other not only for purely physical reasons—like men being attracted to the beautiful Angela or my being attracted to Mike only at the dance when he held me close—but also out of a deeper need.

Chapter 6

Schooldays & Sundays

My first school was Miss Minella's Nursery, of which I have no memory beyond its exterior looks. Located on Thompson Street, its orangey-red bricks looked cheerful alongside a small fenced-in playground. The neighborhood mothers revered Miss Minella. Then I went to P. S. 8 on King Street for kindergarten. How I hated that place. The school was a massive brick building, cold and impersonal. It had grimy windows and was probably typical of New York City public schools of the time.

Because I was a very slow eater, a few older girls in eighth grade had to sit with me until I finished my lunch while the rest of the kindergarteners went back to class. The cavernous lunchroom was dimly lit. It had extremely high ceilings and bars on the windows. The eighth graders had no interest in babysitting me: the girls were more interested in flirting with the boys. This was all to the good from my point of view because they forgot about me and I could eat my apple undisturbed by their ministrations.

These were all tough kids, or least rough spoken, not like the kids I was used to.

I remember little beyond that except that I had a little red corduroy suit I wore to school on a day I had a bad cold. My handkerchief with my grandmother's tatting at the edges was tucked into my sleeve. We were crayoning a square box, drawn on a piece of paper, with layers of different colors. Between my very runny nose, the difficulty I was having retrieving my handkerchief, and my drawing 'out of the box' I impressed no one that day.

That I should remember that red suit or a pink plaid Easter suit my mother bought me one year around the same time suggests that I was beginning to think of myself as an individual who had her own style.

I also enjoyed dressing in my mother's old clothes. I walked in her shoes—a pair of high heels with a delicate mauve lace top—snuggled in her fox jacket, and donned a red felt hat with a feather at a jaunty angle.

Finally my mother switched me to Our Lady of Mercy, a small school on Washington Square South, where New York University's Law School is now located. Though my father was anti-clerical due to a priest's boxing him on his ear in grammar school hard enough to cause partial hearing loss, he nonetheless sent me to this Catholic school. It was a school of about a hundred kids in eight grades, run by a French order of nuns. It was on a human scale—not the gigantic size of P. S. 8—and, for the most part, the nuns, if not great educators, were humane. My father had probably looked into this aspect of the school and the nuns' gentle ways had quelled his doubts about religious schools.

I still remember the wind-up phonograph that ran on hand power instead of electricity. Though the large indoor playroom on the first floor was dark, it was cozy with its low ceiling and built-in benches against one wall.

When the school closed to make way for NYU's Law School, I attended St. Joseph Academy at 20 Washington Square North. This school had sophisticated nuns as well as students with broad interests and some parents who were making their mark in New York.

One interesting student who grew up to be First Deputy Mayor of New York City in 1975 under Mayor Abraham Beame was John Zuccotti. A tall, broad built boy with a shock of black hair that always fell across his forehead, John was very interested, even then, in politics. His interests at the time ran more to the international scene. We had a current events bulletin board set up at the back of the class with world maps displayed. During this class John would lumber to the back of the classroom—he had flat feet which I think was responsible for the way he walked—and stand at the bulletin board and start discoursing on Iran. This was the early fifties when the new Shah of Iran was being put into power. (When my father came home from work during this time, he'd always ask, "What do you think of the Iranian situation?") As John's speech would go on, his voice would rise with excitement. If one of the boys made an objection to one of his statements—we girls didn't dare interrupt him—he'd become even more exuberant and talk even louder, waving his arms and pounding the map. Sister Ellen, our eighth grade teacher enjoyed John's antics. He enlivened the class and showed his passion for world affairs. Imagine my surprise when twenty years later, I read in the *New York Times* words to the effect that the usual calm John Zuccotti had displayed his customary reasonable approach to a city problem.

John had entered politics when Mayor John Lindsay appointed him to the New York City Planning Commission in 1971 and two years later made him Chairman of the Commission.

On the other hand, Geraldine DeSapio, Carmine DeSapio's daughter, never showed any interest in current events. A slim girl tending towards the beautiful with her jet-black hair, dark eyes and a rosy olive complexion, Geraldine never put herself forward. She was well liked by both boys and girls—maybe especially by the boys. She was wary of such attentions because of her father's rising position in Tammany Hall, the reputation of which, we learned in school, had been tainted by Boss Tweed. Geraldine always seemed to wither under that fact.

She was probably right to be wary of certain attentions. One boy, who attended a Village parochial school located near ours, was blatant in his interest in Geraldine as a girl friend who could promote his desired entry into politics through her father. Always polite to him, she nonetheless rebuffed his interest in her. The rest of us sniggered at his self-interest and seeming devotion whenever he came around to Washington Square Park to see Geraldine after school.

Tammany Hall's power and influence had waned in the thirties and forties. In 1943, Carmine DeSapio was named district leader for lower Greenwich Village. By 1949 he had gained enough power to be named boss of Tammany Hall, which, under his leadership, began to re-emerge as an important influence in New York City politics. By the fifties DeSapio was the kingmaker of New York politics. In 1953 the power of Tammany led to the defeat of Mayor Impelliteri by Robert Wagner. In 1954 he brokered the nomination of Averill Harriman for governor, an act that Eleanor Roosevelt never forgave him for. She had wanted her own son to run for governor and later she was instrumental, along with Mayor Edward Koch, in dethroning DeSapio. Harriman went on to become Secretary of State. During DeSapio's career, he supported the Fair Employment Practices Law, New York City rent control, and lowering the voting age to eighteen.

I only met him once when I attended Geraldine's home party on Charlton Street, not far from where I lived, for her eleventh birthday. But I remember the cut of his jib to this day. When Carmine DeSapio entered their apartment, he exuded energy. He was tall, slim and handsome—not like so many of our fathers who were short, portly and ordinary looking. When we were introduced to him, his eyes shining through his gold-rimmed glasses—his eye disease had not yet progressed to the stage where he needed to wear dark glasses—he greeted us all by name and chatted for a few minutes. And then he left. A whirlwind had come and gone.

Gerry and I attended high school together as well, continuing the tradition of staying with the same order of nuns as we moved on to the next level of studies. She disliked anyone fawning over her because of who her father was. And this dislike included some of the nuns. At graduation, the nuns invented a new award to give to Gerry, something to do with school spirit or good citizenship. The award embarrassed her terribly. She promptly gave up all thoughts of continuing with this order of nuns in college and attended a Catholic college on Staten Island.

Another memorable classmate was Sonny. That was how he was known, instead of his very un-American name of Rocco. The name Sonny suited his looks better than Rocco that to my mind demanded a commanding physical presence. Sonny was short and baby-faced with very soft pale skin that held no trace of an emerging beard. Yet by eighth grade his voice had completely changed to a bass register with none of the awkward squeals or cracks that plagued the other boys.

Sonny was also the smartest and richest boy in the class. He received a ten-dollar a week allowance at a time when most of us felt blest to receive a dollar. He had been born late in the life of his parents and his doting sister, who was at least ten years older than he, seemed to be his main caretaker.

Sonny used his intellect to promote two of his favorite theses; one that God did not exist and the second that if money were re-distributed the same people would become rich and the same people would be poor. He took every opportunity to argue these propositions and unlike the rest of us, he had no fear in challenging the nuns or even a visiting priest.

Sister Ellen's approach to Sonny was based less on arguing the issues with him than in treating him indulgently as a smart child who needed to sprout his wings. This was an excellent strategy for it reduced Sonny from a serious thinker to a spoiled kid who liked to challenge authority, thus safeguarding the beliefs of the rest of us, Sister Ellen's charges.

He loved dominating by the power of his mind and he sought out girls with whom he could argue his positions, often in a witty, low-keyed way. One day as he walked me home, we spent the time debating back and forth some of his favorite propositions. I loved the intellectual stimulation and we each were attracted to the other.

He occasionally came over to our house in the evening to play poker with my brother and his friends when they were at an age when they needed to try out harmless male activities. Years later, my brother told me that Sonny had gone off the deep end and had become almost a Nazi. Perhaps Sister Ellen should have taken him more seriously.

High School

My high school, located at 42 East 84th Street in Manhattan, had eighty-three girls. Some of the students came from 'feeder' schools, where the Sisters of Charity encouraged their eighth graders to attend another Sisters of Charity school. Others of the students were the daughters of South American diplomats. These daughters of diplomats were usually engaged to be married. The school seemed a protective environment for them while they perfected their English. While I tried to befriend them, we had little in common. They weren't interested in boys in the same way we were. After all, they were engaged and we girls were interested in meeting boys to date: we attended basketball games of the local boys' high schools, an occasional football game, and dramatic offerings, giggling away at a boy Portia in *Merchant of Venice*. Marriage was far from our minds.

In sophomore and junior year, two other foreign students attended my high school. They were two sisters from Panama who spoke excellent English and were not engaged. Besides being a lot of fun, they had a good-looking brother who had once posed as an Indian for a priest's flyer to raise money for an Indian mission.

Unlike us with our New York accents dropping 'r's and

rushing over 'l's, the sisters spoke mellifluously, not quite rolling their 'r's, but giving them their full due along with their liquid 'l's. I rushed to imitate them. Those sounds were so delicious.

My father didn't always appreciate my desire to speak well. When I was in eighth grade he quizzed me on the English accent I was developing. Surprised, I realized that I must have unconsciously been imitating one of my best friends, Judy, who had escaped from Germany with her family. They had first gone to London before gaining entry into America. Although she wasn't Jewish, her father, who was a doctor, was and they had had to flee.

I expected that Judy would be traumatized by such events, but she never spoke about her past. Except for her banana curls in the style of Shirley Temple, she seemed like just another ordinary teenager to us girls, but one with an English accent.

Once, she and I went on a double date with her boyfriend and his cousin. Judy had met this boy through friends of friends of ours from a different and poorer neighborhood. Her boyfriend was a good-looking fellow, but he didn't seem like the type boy Judy would like. He wasn't as smart or as sophisticated as she and he spoke with a strong New York accent. The other thing that distinguished him was that he had a wooden leg that squeaked when he walked—which he did with some difficulty. Perhaps he asked her out because girls from his own neighborhood shunned him due to his leg. Given

Judy's background, she would be loath to shun someone for being different. Judy herself had never dated before this, perhaps because of her British accent and banana curls. She may have accepted his daytime invitation to try out her feminine skills. She was no less interested in boys than the rest of us young teenagers.

Judy was very close to her mother and confided in her. Her mother was a wise and gentle woman whom I could imagine counseling her daughter to go out with the boy once and see how it went. Although Judy was pleasant and sociable during that day, conversation was somewhat stilted and strained. I don't think she ever went out with the boy again and I had no interest in seeing his cousin on another date either.

In high school, I enjoyed dramatics and glee club. As a freshman for our Easter play I received the lead part playing a young boy who had seen Christ crucified. On opening night, my friends sat in the front row of the auditorium and I could hear one, who was a master of undercutting people through humor, whisper to her seatmate how funny I looked. Her laugh was infectious and I feared I would start laughing too when I was supposed to be crying over what I had seen. I buried my head in my hands and succeeded in suppressing an eruption of laughter.

I loved writing as much as I loved dramatics and my classmates elected me assistant editor of the school newspaper. To contain printing costs, the editor and I, in order to have a right justified margin, had to fit the letters of each line into squares, leaving greater or lesser spaces between words to achieve that end. This was a long way from computers or even electric typewriters, but we patiently did the work to achieve a good-looking result.

My life was hardly all work and no play. High school friends who lived near the school on the Upper East Side often invited me to be their guest at Miss Blaugh's dancing school. Attended mainly by Protestant boys from private schools in the area, the dances were very different from the ones held at Catholic schools. The emphasis here was on sophistication. Generally the boys were more iconoclastic than the Catholic boys and I enjoyed being with them and eventually dating some. One who became the love of my life in high school was Dick. He attended Collegiate High School. Of Dutch background, he had the rosy cheeks to prove it. An outstanding football player, he enjoyed playing the drums. When I showed my daughter a photo of him from that time playing the drums, she dubbed him the little drummer boy.

A young nun at the high school whom we girls confided in was sure I'd lose my soul in dating this Protestant. Before meeting him she must have pictured him with horns. Catholics like her, who went into the convent right after high school, often had never met a Protestant. When she finally saw him at a high school dance I attended with him, she quickly reversed her opinion. Dick could be described as good looking and, as we said then, clean-cut. In meeting him, all her fears evaporated. This immediate turn around made me realize how truly sheltered she was.

Dick was going through a difficult time at home. His mother was an alcoholic and his parents were going through a divorce. We went 'steady' for almost two years, and though I tried to be supportive during this time, we eventually broke up. We had different visions for our futures. Because of his home situations, Dick really had no vision for a future. I was focused on going to college. He joined the Navy.

We went out one more time during his Navy stint. He was trying to win me back and took me to the restaurant, Tables on the Green, to woo me. Though the restaurant, situated in Central Park, was in a very romantic setting, I felt nothing for this boy whom I thought I had loved so much in high school.

Dick called one more time after I had graduated from college to ask me out. By that time I had to tell him I was engaged.

College

In college at Mt. St. Vincent-on-Hudson in Riverdale, New York, I continued my interest in dramatics, where each year the main play presented was a Shakespearean one. As a sophomore in an all girls' school, I played Rosencrantz or Guildenstern in *Hamlet*—they were certainly Tweedle-Dee and Tweedle-Dum so that I no longer remember whom I played. On opening night, my partner and I appeared on stage in our short tunics and tights. A low, but unmistakable, hum of laughter swept across the audience. Our brocade tunics, it seemed, stood out from our bosoms so that we looked pregnant. No more such faux pas occurred in subsequent plays and by senior year, I was elected vice president of the dramatics club.

My interest in writing also continued. I contributed stories, poems and articles to the college's literary magazine. While pleased that I had been elected to an office in the dramatics club, I really wanted to be editor of the literary magazine. The day of the vote I was sorely tempted to vote for myself, but forbore doing so. Thanks goodness I had, because except for my vote, everyone else had voted for me.

I enjoyed every aspect of being editor from soliciting articles to overseeing the artwork to working on the business end. I spent a lot of time on the design of the journal, introducing artwork that bled into the margins and paying attention to the font used in the headlines.

I believe I was the first Italian American to become editor of the quarterly magazine. Irish American girls had dominated its pages in earlier years. After the first issue, a retired English professor, Blanche Mary Kelly, wrote the faculty advisor that the editor, me, couldn't write. Instead of accepting her judgment, I chalked up her evaluation to prejudice against Italians. Whether this was true or not, I'll never know, but that was my interpretation at the time.

Because she was of my mother's generation or perhaps even earlier, I believed that she had a prejudice against Italians, which my mother had experienced at the hands of the Irish. I made a distinction between her generation and my generation of Irish people. Many of my best friends were Irish American and I felt no bias from them. As a matter of fact, dear Reader, I married an Irish American although in the interest of full disclosure, I have to reveal that we divorced after a decade and a half of marriage.

Prof. Kelly's comment probably caused me to work even harder on the magazine generally so as to be sure of proving her wrong. I don't remember consciously working on improving my own writing but instead continued in my own way to express myself. When I think of my level of self-confidence at that age, I'm staggered, having spent a lot of my grammar school years and my adult life with great doubts about my abilities. As a matter of fact, in eighth grade I had been chosen to be one of the students in my class to interview the editor of the *Villager,* the local newspaper before the *Village Voice* was founded. Too shy to engage in such an undertaking, I conveniently got 'sick' on the day we were to go.

The year that I was editor of my college magazine, the magazine won first place for form and content for the first time in a national college competition. I had been vindicated and enjoyed this victory immensely.

In my high school, only French was offered as a foreign language. In college I wanted to take Italian. My college advisor asked me if I intended to go to graduate school. I told her that I was interested in doing so. She then told me that I'd have to take French. Being among the first in my family to attend college, I didn't know that this wasn't true and so I continued my French studies. But one year my schedule was such that I could audit an Italian literature course on Dante and other heavyweights of early Italian literature.

I found that if I read their words out loud I could understand their poetry. Somehow my grandmother's words, though a dialect, rang in my ears and I could make the translations from that dialect to Tuscan Italian.

The professor who taught us had a charming Italian accent when he spoke English. He wasn't much older than we. He had piercing blue eyes and though his hair was a bit thin, we were all, if not in love with him, in awe of him. And he was in love with one of the young women, who was engaged, in our class. Towards the end of the year, Rosemary showed me the poetry that the professor had written her. In his poetry to her he had focused on the hated engagement ring on her finger.

Almost twenty years after this class, I ran into the Italian professor at a conference. He greeted me warmly and at the end of the conference he presented me with a poem he had written to me. Flattered by such attention, we made a date to get together for lunch the next time I was in New York City. At the time I was living in Providence, but I regularly traveled to New York to visit my aging, widowed mother who still lived in the same apartment where I grew up.

I introduced Joseph to my mother of Mary Pickford fame. She was still a beautiful woman who at age seventy-five continued to dye her hair blond. Joseph charmed her and after some conversation, he and I went to lunch in a little restaurant on MacDougal Street. The restaurant had a glass-enclosed area where he and I sat and talked over a long, slow lunch.

I found him pompous and without decency. He 'lectured' me on the derivation of pupil from the French, 'poupée.' He told me how he had won a prestigious poetry prize by being nominated by a past recipient with whom, though she was twenty years older than he, he had had a long relationship. When I asked him where she was now, he was dismissive of her not in the sense of not wanting me to feel she was still in his life, but because he truly had no more interest in her once he had gained what he wanted. It was so cold and calculating I had no interest in seeing him again. Thereafter when I visited New York, I never let him know.

After many months of putting him off about seeing him again, I learned from my mother that Joseph had called her to invite her to lunch. She was reluctant to go. I encouraged her to accept, because despite his shortcomings, which might not be apparent to my mother, my mother would enjoy his continental charm and companionship. I convinced her and a week or so later, off they went to lunch.

I called my mother the next day to find out how her 'date' had gone. She agreed that he was charming. But then she said, "You know, Carol, if I had let him, I think he wanted to sleep with me."

I had hardly expected him to make such a proposition to my mother who was twenty years older than he. Ah, true love, I thought, in the time of drought, but all I said was, "Well mom, you're still a very attractive woman." She made no response.

Sundays

I loved Sundays because on that day, after church, my brother Tom and I visited my Auntie Rose and Lillie, her daughter and my godmother. They lived right across the street from our church, St. Anthony of Padua, so it was very convenient.

After church we walked up four flights of stairs with depressions in the middle of the treads from decades of use. The poorly lit hallway had dark brown walls. With some minor misgivings my brother and I eyed the defunct dumb waiter still set into the far wall. The dumb waiter, which had been used to lower garbage to the basement, held an eerie fascination. At one and the same time I wanted to ride up the dumb waiter to the fourth floor, but I also feared its dark claustrophobic interior.

At their door Auntie Rose, long apron neatly tied over her housedress and Lillie, red hair in a short bob, welcomed us with hugs, kisses and smiles. We entered the kitchen with its old-fashioned saltbox hanging to the right of the stove.

Knowing that we loved almonds, Lillie shelled mounds of them for us—as many as we wanted. I sat by the huge window overlooking Houston Street all the way to Sixth Avenue, munching almonds and watching the world go by. It doesn't take much to make a child happy—unconditional love and a favorite food.

During the war years, their window had an Army star hanging in it because Auntie Rose's son John was in the Army. Once he was discharged and married, he, his wife and their son visited as well, living as they did only a few blocks away. John, or as we all called him, Eugene—my mother, having a 'thing' about names, supposedly renamed him—always had jokes to tell. He was a very good storyteller, adding dialects and body movements, so that we always laughed a lot at his stories. In my opinion Lillie was just as good a storyteller as her brother, but, being in an Italian family, she didn't get the attention she deserved for her joke telling. As a matter of fact, she herself added to the mythic reputation of Eugene as a great joke teller by always laughing appreciatively, praising his talent, and taking a back seat to him.

After we had our fill of almonds, Lillie served us her meatballs, sitting on a plate in a small pool of sauce. In our family her meatballs were legendary for their tenderness and taste. Although years later I took down the recipe as I watched her make them, I'm convinced that the secret ingredient was Lillie's love, for mine never tasted as good. How I loved Lillie for all the love she showered on me.

We returned home stuffed, hardly hungry for our mid-afternoon main meal of macaroni, meatballs, sausages, braciole (my favorite: a roll of thin beef stuffed with garlic, cheese, and parsley and simmered in tomato sauce), artichokes stuffed with chopped parsley and garlic, roast beef, salad, and fruit for dessert. At night we each went into the kitchen as hunger hit us and ate leftovers from the earlier meal; then we listened to the radio—Jack Benny and Fred Allen's programs were the usual. My favorite was Jack Benny with his frugal persona, Stanley Steamer car, and ensemble cast of his wife Mary, and butler Rochester. I particularly liked Jack Benny's Ahaheim...and Cuc-ca-monga train station bit. Fred Allen's dryer humor was perhaps too sophisticated for someone my age, though I appreciated his cast of characters and various sound effects.

During one period of time on Sundays, I remember my father taking us to Carlo's drug store on Bleecker Street for a banana split. Perhaps he picked us up after we visited with Auntie Rose and Lillie. My brother and I sat at the long counter and happily ate our banana splits, our father sitting alongside us, watching with pleasure as we enjoyed a treat that he as a child could only dream about.

If I thoroughly enjoyed Sundays during the day, Sunday evenings were more problematic. As a child, I had a fear of the dark. At bedtime, my door had to remain open and the light on the long table in the living room, which shined at an angle diagonal to my bedroom door, had to remain on.

Every Sunday evening, when my parents attended the newsreels in Times Square, I'd get particularly nervous. My grandmother would babysit us, but that wasn't sufficient to allay my fears of the dark. I'd imagine seeing people walking by the darkened window of the bedroom. Or the lights from cars passing by would project strange shadows on the walls and ceiling. Having been brought up in a religious atmosphere at school, I often thought it was Jesus walking up and down in front of the drawn blinds. That scared me the most. It was heavy having God in the room with me. I'd call to my grandmother who would come in and I'd tell her something or other about not being able to sleep. I never mentioned that Jesus was in the room with me. Who would have believed me? Not even I would. I knew He couldn't be, but still, still...I quaked with fear.

Even as an adult, I was very sensitive to suggestion. When I was thirty-something, I saw the film, *Jaws*, and after that I never again swam straight out into the ocean, imagining sharks waiting to grab me. I used to love swimming straight out into the ocean without end. Swimming away from the shore gave me such a sense of freedom. It was the same feeling I had when I was pumping myself on a swing high above the trees or when I hung from the monkey bars by my knees. At those times as a child, I was fearless and free.

Chapter 7

Back to the Beginnings

The lives of my maternal grandmother and paternal grandfather (dead a year before I was born) are really where my story begins. All the major events of the twentieth century touched their lives to greater and lesser degrees and indirectly touched my life as well. While my relatives' and my experiences constitute a microcosm of the Italian experience in America, they occurred within the broader context of American and world history. Some of these events include my maternal and paternal grandparents leaving Italy due to the Risorgimento's failures to effect reforms in southern Italy; my uncle marching on Washington to agitate for the bonus that the government promised World War I soldiers; the worldwide flu epidemic of 1918 causing the death of my aunt's first husband and the subsequent hard life she led; my mother finally becoming a citizen in 1927, twenty years after emigrating from Italy, due perhaps to the Red Scare, anarchism, Sacco and Vanzetti and the restrictive immigration laws of 1924; the stock market crash of 1929 causing my father to sell his GM stock to help his brother out of financial difficulties; McCarthyism causing me many a troubled sleep after I unknowingly signed a Communist petition; the reemergence of a powerful Tammany Hall with an Italian-American leader whom I would meet at his daughter's birthday party; the Smith bill, which became the Alien Registration Act, leading me to great introspection about my grandmother's place in America; and the aftermath of World War II and fascism when my family mailed letters and packages to help keep Italy non-Communist.

Perhaps of lesser import on the public level were the introduction of settlement houses, where I took classes and was introduced to a broader world, and the initiatives of the food reformers, their legacy partly responsible for the lumpy mashed potatoes my mother made.

I have little to relate about my father's family since I never knew my grandfather or my father's brothers, all three dead before I was born. My father was generally silent concerning his parents and brothers. Because my teacher assigned my class to interview our parents about the Depression, my father told me a story about one of his brothers who had been among the World War I veterans who had marched on Washington in July of 1932. In great need of money, they wanted their cash war service bonuses well before the 1945 date set to collect them. The government refused to give it to them. Many veterans left

Washington in defeat, but of those who remained the government violently drove them out of D. C.

My father was rather silent about his own childhood. The stories he told were often about the poverty of his upbringing, though a few were not of this nature. When he was nine or so, he remembers gleefully sneaking into the cellar of his tenement with his friend Joey and opening each spigot from every cask of homemade wine which the building's tenants stored there. Both boys drank their fill. But the story ends, not on a note of delight, but with his ruefulness at having gotten drunk and sick from the excess of wine.

Another story involved his sitting on his stoop and making his own crystal radio set and how he delicately moved the crystal to bring in the different stations. Crystal radios could be made, then as now, with simple supplies, most of which could be found in the home. Yet with this story, too, was the undercurrent of sadness that he was unable to study further in this burgeoning field. Electronics attracted him, so much so that when he bought our first TV, my father spent many hours adjusting the round test pattern that came on the screen when no program was showing. He wanted the pattern to hold perfectly, pulling neither to right nor left. This drove us all crazy since we didn't see the irregularities he saw.

According to my mother, my father's father was a handsome man. The one photo I saw of him confirms that. My mother said that he was a genial man whom she liked very much. He sold fruits and vegetables from a cart. His first wife died and his second-wife, Anna Maria, was the person my father called to when he was in pain. Born a *contadino* as his birth certificate notes in 1852, my paternal grandfather died in 1937 so that he only saw his grandson, my brother Tom. When as an adult I saw his birth certificate with the description *contadino*, peasant, written on it, I understood the static culture of the country my grandfather had been born into.

Growing up, I had always expected at some point to visit Italy. I was brought up on tales of all the residents of my grandmother's home town descending upon the train station with flowers in hand to greet my cousin Gloria when she arrived in the late nineteen forties to visit. Memories of the help we had given the relatives after the war were fresh in Italians' minds as was American abundance with its Marshall Plan and Fulbright scholarships.

Italy has always exerted a hold over me, despite my parents and grandparents conflicted feelings about the country. For my grandmother it both pulled her back, returning as she did in 1912, and pushed her forth once again nine months later. While my mother inherited her mother's ultimate rejection of the country—my mother never wanted to visit and spoke of her relatives there in an embarrassed way as 'country yokels'—she, having access to other information about Italy, knew that it comprised more than the poverty her family had known. She saw its natural beauty in pictures; she learned of its high art; she heard Italian opera.

These are the images of Italy she passed on to me and which I delved into through traveling there as soon as I was able, right after college, when tour companies offered cheap trips to college students on re-fitted World War II boats. For $340 during the summer, the S.S. Rotterdam took over at least a thousand students, four to a room with bunk beds, and three meals a day, served by Indonesian waiters. For another $1,000, covering food, hotel, transportation and museum fees, I toured most of Europe for three full months, two and a half weeks spent in Italy. Despite tour companies' definition of Italy as Pompeii and above (so that I never saw the South of my ancestors), I fell in love with the country, as I knew I would. I was predisposed.

But on that trip, I was not primed nor predisposed, to visit my grandmother's relatives, some of whom we had stayed in touch with, if very sporadically, over the years. It would be thirteen more years before I visited Lauropoli in Calabria, twenty-eight years for Anzi in Basilicata, and another seventeen years before I explored the larger region of the South, Calabria, Basilicata and Puglia.

My initial interest in Italy lay in first seeing its high culture—I had always enjoyed viewing works of art—so that after graduating college, I did the typical 'grand tour' pilgrimage, visiting Rome, Florence, Venice and other Northern towns. Florence became my favorite city, as much for its beauty as for its people, clever conversationalists on all sorts of matters: on my twenty-first birthday, three handsome Italian boys, dressed more in the style of American prep students, with their navy blazers, than as Italians (at that time Italians most often wore slacks and sweaters), accompanied my two girlfriends and me on a leisurely walk through Florence. Their English was excellent; our Italian passable. They differed from the Casanovian stereotype in that they behaved like perfect gentlemen. It was a lovely way to spend a significant birthday. What was there not to love about Italy?

But now I wanted to immerse myself in Basilicata and Calabria, where my grandparents were born. Basilicata particularly interested me because the region was among the poorest of the Italian provinces. Its inhabitants, like my grandfather, who was born in the town of Anzi, were among the first to emigrate from Italy, about 1882 or 1883, than the inhabitants of other provinces in Italy.

Basilicata

Basilicata is the 'instep' of the Italian boot. On my first visit to the mountain town of Anzi in Basilicata (a half hour by car south of Potenza, which lies east of Naples), I was struck by its height—at its pinnacle I felt as if there was no demarcation between the earth and the clouds. As I looked down at the valley—the valley that my grandfather had probably farmed—I was constantly pulled back up to the sky and the clouds and to a thought similar to one expressed in Max Frankel's *Man's Search for Meaning*: how beautiful the visible world is.

The winding streets, rising ever upward, on that visit, seemed emptied of young people. An occasional old person could be seen standing at her door—they were always women—dressed in black and eager for company. In the town itself there seemed to be only pale yellow stucco houses and the church, shut for repairs due to the 1981 earthquake ten years earlier.

By the time of my visit to Basilicata in 2007, I had read Carlo Levi's 1947 book, *Christ Stopped at Eboli,* about the area, which made me extremely interested in seeing what the region was like now. Levi, an anti-Fascist, had been exiled there in the 1930s and wrote about his experiences. Though the events in the book occurred in the thirties, I found the book compelling in that I suspected that the region had not changed much from when my grandfather had lived there. I was eager to see what the area was like now

I learned that after World War II peasant uprisings resulted in land reform where 12,000 small plots (about an acre to an acre and a half each) were distributed to the peasants in Basilicata's Metapontean region, called the California of Italy due to its fruit and vegetable production. The government also tried industrialization, but corruption and various boondoggles caused industrial initiatives to be unsuccessful. Finally with

Italy's entry into the European Union industrialization succeeded because the EU demanded doing away with the timeworn practices of creating fake pensioners and other such fraudulent practices. And so in the 1990s the building of the Melfi Fiat plant became a success story. Basilicata has oil in its south central section, but limited transportation and the means to refine the crude oil has restricted development of this resource. It's also rich in water, a rarity in the South.

Matera, which became a city in early medieval times, was one of my first stops on this exploration of Basilicata. Once the shame of Italy, it is now a tourist attraction. In the 1950s, its shame was that some of its people were living in caves without electricity or water. These caves were reputed to be the world's oldest continuously lived-in caves, dating from Neolithic times. The government finally built public housing for the people and cleared the caves. Now the caves have been gentrified. Electricity and running water were installed so that young wealthier people were attracted to the area, which now has its own charm. Why the government couldn't have put in electricity and water when the poor lived there is the age-old question of how governments, in removing the poor, help the rich.

On my next stop I detoured to the neighboring region of Puglia to the port city of Bari (from *barion,* meaning house or group of houses), which developed a commercial presence even earlier than Matera. As early as the second century B. C., ancient Rome, which had conquered the Samnites in Bari in 334 B. C., was able to control piracy in the region, and Bari's commercial port developed and grew.

Trajan eventually ordered the construction of the Via Trajana to supplement the Appian Way. By cutting across the peninsula at a narrower point through Brindisi, Trajan's road shortened the land route from Rome to Bari by two weeks, making its port even more desirable. A portion of Trajan's Way, which eventually went all the way to northwestern Spain, is uncovered in Bari and can be seen today.

I continued on in Puglia to Lecce, noted for its Baroque architecture. But it is Baroque architecture with a southern twist. Due to the softness of the stone used in Lecce, the Baroque style of the north had a much freer mode of expression, concentrating on decoration, with pinecones, pomegranates, grapes, and cherries abounding along with other plant life, such as garlands with seeds illustrating the fertility of the area. Horses, naked women and dozens of children were sculpted. To me the emphasis on children—romping, jumping, playing—covering almost every inch of the columns of its churches and cathedral are indicative of the love of children that marks so much of the south.

Calabria

My second trip to Italy occurred after I was married. My then husband was on a sabbatical from Brown University and we toured Italy with our two children, showing them the high culture we enjoyed so much. But on this trip to Calabria in 1972 we also visited the same relatives who had greeted my cousin Gloria with flowers twenty years earlier. But by then, over twenty years later, the novelty of visiting Americans had worn off. As I was discovering the Italy of my ancestors, I wanted it to discover me, but, to my disappointment, no hometown greeting with flowers awaited me as it had my cousin Gloria.

I made my way to the Records Office where I saw the wrinkled card on which my grandmother's emigration was recorded. The carabinieri telephoned my mother's cousin whose name, Francesco Aloisi, my mother had given me before I left. He came to meet us and took us to see my grandmother's sisters and other relatives. Francesco had taught school and my poorer relatives, my grandmother's sister Anna Maria and her children, greeted him by the appellation, "Professor." He lapped it up and they practically kissed his hand. I was appalled by such obvious class distinctions, especially given the fact that it existed so overtly and naturally among relatives.

A variety of life styles existed among the various strands of the family from the 'poor' sister, Anna Maria, to Concetta whose family, due to her husband's working in America a half century before, was doing fairly well, to the comfortable Guerrieris, my grandmother's husband's side of the family, who owned a jewelry and gift store. The area of town where they all lived was unremarkable. It was the newer part of town with streets laid out in an orderly, unpicturesque grid.

After visiting with family, I walked around the town a bit to get a sense of it, viewing the piazza. Nothing remarkable distinguished it, a few trees, some benches, a tobacco shop. Some rough looking young men hung about along with some older unshaven men and one who roamed about talking to himself. Amid the streets of the old town, I found the fountain with sulphuric waters that my grandmother had praised so highly. It was the only thing she praised about Italy. My impression of the town, Lauropoli, was of a tired, worn-out backwater to live.

It wasn't until my third visit over thirty years later to the province of Calabria that I discovered the culture of the region itself. At that later time I was more interested in learning about the area and its history than in visiting relatives. (Three years earlier I had been invited to give two lectures at a language institute in St. Demetrio al Corona, a Byzantine town whose inhabitants still lapsed into the ancient Albanian dialect from the sixteenth century). Although it was very near my grandmother's hometown, I didn't visit any of the relatives because I felt the connection had been severed long ago with the death of my grandmother's sisters.)

Having earlier in my life experienced inner conflict about my Italian background, I had now reached a point of wanting to immerse myself in the culture of the South. I still was not free of viewing the area in the same way as George Gissing, in his 1897 visit to Calabria did: "One remembers all they have suffered, all they have achieved in spite of wrong. Brute races have flung themselves, one after another, on this sweet and glorious land; conquest and slavery, from age to age, have been the people's lot. Tread where one will, the soil has been drenched with blood." But I was to see that this was no longer the reality that existed in Calabria.

Calabria is the region of Italy south of Basilicata that comprises the 'toes' and 'sole' of Italy. Its population today is over two million, yet what strikes one about its topography of sea on both sides and mountains in the middle, is the sense of isolated towns on the hilltops of the Sila Mountains with no roads connecting them. It's no wonder that one contemporary scholar has thus far found 3,000 dialects spoken in Calabria. Another scholar made up a chart of concentric circles representing the dialects of all of Italy with standard Italian at the center. He found that the Calabrian dialects were closer to standard Italian because Calabrian dialects adhered to influences from the Greeks and Romans who conquered them in ancient times (or even from the Byzantine conquest in the 6th century A. D. or Greeks fleeing the Turks during their invasion of Greece) while Northern Italy had greater

171

foreign influences, such as German and French.

In ancient times the area was known as Magna Grecia with Sybari, Crotone, and Locri some of the Greek cities in the area. In the Peloponnesian Wars of 431 to 404 B. C. the independent Greek towns in Calabria, using the wood from Calabrian trees for their boats, fought with the victorious Spartans against Athens. Sparta came out of the wars weakened, thus indirectly preparing the way for Rome to conquer the region some two hundred years later.

On my most recent visit, I first toured Gerace, a Calabrian town founded by refugees from Locri in the ninth century. This town houses the oldest Byzantine church in Calabria, the tiny ninth-century church of St. John Chrysostom, with its two doors, one for men and one for women. Its thirteenth century church of St. Francis holds beautiful marble mosaics replete with scenes from daily life, such as two monks, with their shadows depicted, playing with a dog, a colorful parrot, two birds eating a fly and a mosquito, and another eating a pomegranate.

Rossano, another Byzantine town flourishing from the eighth to the eleventh centuries, holds the earliest illustrated Gospel in the world, the Codex Purpureus Rossanensis, dating from the sixth century. Its pages' purple background color derives from the mollusk. It is theorized that the Gospel was drawn in Syria because in the scene with the moneychangers, the bulls are Syrian bulls with their distinctive horns.

I visited Cosenza and stood in the piazza where, in 1844, peasant uprisings occurred. I walked its streets and saw all the ateliers of artisans, making shoes, repairing ancient tapestries and working on lace.

I saw acres of greenhouses for raspberries, which a priest introduced ten years ago, to help unemployed and disadvantaged youth. Kiwis were also being cultivated, moving Calabria away from its dependence on its one-crop mode of agriculture. Bergamo trees with their citrus fruit are everywhere in the region. A citrus hybrid, its parts are used to make products as disparate as Earl Grey tea, a liqueur, and perfume.

I learned of how the mayor in the early 1960s, Giacomo Mancini, was instrumental in having a national park developed in the area and in building a university there so that the Calabrese students would be able to attend college. I also learned of the Calabrian Zimbabe mission for sustainable agriculture. This charity to which Calabrians donate monies made me realize that the south of my imagination was a south that thankfully no longer existed. It was now a south that was on the giving, not the receiving, end of charity. And yet I still needed to identify with my grandmother's life as a final attempt to be free from its haunting of me.

I knew about the life of my grandmother from what I observed about her, from talking to her three children, visiting her home town and meeting two of her sisters and their extended families. Steeped in reading about the

Italians and the Italian Americans for over thirty years, I've imagined scenes reflecting my maternal ancestors' lives. Books such as Norman Douglas's *Old Calabria,* Robert Foerster's 1919 book, *The Italian Emigration of our Time,* about the Italian immigrants, George Gissings's *By the Ionian Sea* and Carlo Levi's *Christ Stopped at Eboli,* are some of the books that formed the basis for my imagination to take flight as well as some information I've learned from relatives.

Italy Imagined

Lauropoli was quiet at that time of day in 1903. The calm descended from Mt. Polino in the north down to the fields further south. Even the old castle at the top of the hill was quiet, but two children, carrying a square screen framed in wood between them, could be seen tripping down the parched road. Occasionally they stopped, laughed, and tried to pull the screening from each other's hands. Dried grapes on top of the screen bounced topsy-turvey until some fell to the ground. The young girl—no more than five—guffawed, but the boy, two years older at most, stopped laughing and looked towards his house, a small whitewashed affair of one story with a sleeping loft above.

Luigi bent down and began scooping up the raisins with both hands. He swept the ones that hadn't fallen to one side of the screen, quickly dusted off the dirt from the others and threw them back onto the screen, all the while glancing towards his front door. Rosa, still giggling, did a little dance around the raisins.

The door opened. Their mother surveyed the scene, strode over to Rosa and grabbed her wrist. "Help your brother," she commanded.

Rosa tried to control her laughter. She looked up at her mother and then quickly knelt down beside her brother, tidying up the mess while she hid her smile behind a lock of dark brown hair tumbling forward onto her face. Her cheek was rosy against her olive skin.

"What am I going to do with you children? Don't you have any sense? I need to feed your baby sister and this is how you help me? What am I going to do with the two of you? What are *we* going to do?"

She moaned. Rosa tiptoed towards her mother and wrapped her arms around her thighs. Teresina shrugged her off and entered the low-ceilinged dwelling. She picked up the six-month old girl whom she had laid down in her cradle. The baby fussed, kicking her little feet and moving her head from one side to the other. Teresina offered her breast and Michelina sucked hungrily. Teresina sighed. How was she to survive with no cooperation from her children? Certainly Luigi should have known better. He was the oldest. What was she to do? Her mother was ailing and neither her sisters nor brother could help her: Concetta's husband had immigrated to America and Anna Maria was Luigi's age.

Teresina remembered how she had nursed Anna Maria

along with Luigi when her mother was too sick to feed her. Teresina's face softened at the memory. She felt so much younger then with Michele still alive and the thrill of her first child, Luigi. She didn't at all mind feeding Anna Maria too. She loved Anna Maria like her own baby—maybe more than this child whom she now rocked—Michelina, born three months after her husband died. It was the bronchitis that killed him. She could still hear his wracking cough irritating his lungs. Not even her prayers could help him. As powerful a *fattura* as she was, she wasn't powerful enough to help her own husband. Teresina sighed again. How she had wished that she would lose this child, but her powers to will it seemed to have left her.

Her husband's customers kept telling her they'd pay her tomorrow...next time...next week...next month for her services. She had taken over her husband's job of grinding wheat, but few people bothered to pay a mere woman. It had been a business that was able to feed them twice a day—a little bread that she baked in the outdoor oven with some oil on top. Sometimes a tomato. Some wine, cheese, a few raisins, a prickly pear. What else could she do?

She blew her nose, put the sleeping baby back in her cradle, lumbered out the door and over to the wheat-grinder. Serafino waited by the stone with his wheat.

"Good day, Serafino," she whispered.

"Hello, Teresina."

She weighed the wheat and told him how much it would cost to grind it.

"I'll pay you once I sell my wheat."

"And how am I to live in the meantime?" she grumbled.

"I'll give you some of my wheat to hold you over."

Teresina sighed and set the animal to begin the grinding. As the animal moved in its inevitable circle, she thought about how Serafino was one of the few men who hadn't migrated to America. The town was becoming a place of women and children, little sparrows who pecked out a living from the sun-baked earth. Soon there would be no wheat to grind.

Luigi finished scooping up the raisins. He straightened up to his full height, placed both hands into the small of his back and stretched. He was tall compared to the other boys his age, tall like his dead father.

He thought about his father. An ache throbbed in the middle of his chest. He turned and looked towards Mt. Polino. The mountain was his anchor—always there watching over him. Sometimes it glistened in the sunshine and he rejoiced with it. At other times, it hid behind the puff clouds, only to re-emerge in its full splendor.

Rosa tugged at her brother's arm. "Luigi, let's go get some prickly pears. OK?"

"Not now, Rosa. I better see if Mama needs help."

Rosa skipped down the sun-baked road towards the cactus plant and began to pluck off the pears. She shoved them into her pocket, turned and raced home.

"Teresina, Teresina," Concetta yelled as she pushed open the front door.

"Paolo met a relative of Michele's...in *L'America*." Concetto stopped long enough to catch her breath. Shorter than her sister, she strongly resembled her despite the ten years difference in age. Concetta looked much younger than Teresina. She didn't have the cares that her sister had. Her husband, working in America, saved his money and sent it home to her to feed the children. They were even saving for a house and maybe some furniture. Concetta patted her dark hair, fixed in a neat bun at the back of her head.

"Father Rossi just finished reading me the letter. Rocco said he's a good man just like your husband. He has a beautiful house in New York. He wants to marry you."

"Marry me?" Teresina asked. She sat stunned in a corner of the dark room.

"Yes, yes. He has three children just like you. He needs someone—a hard worker—to look after them and he'll take care of you and your children."

"Who is he?"

"He's an in-law of Michele's cousin. A good man," she repeated.

"Why would he want me and my three children?"

"He has children too. You could take care of them while you take care of your own. You wouldn't have to worry about anything," Concetta pressed.

"I don't want to go to America. What do I know about that place or the people?"

"You could learn."

"Why do you want me to leave, to go away from the only place I've known? I don't see you running off to America."

Concetta stared at her sister, annoyed. Then she thought better of it and smiled. "How could I go to *L'America*? Where would we get the money? You know Rocco and I are saving it for a house."

"And where would I get the money? And how would I get it for the children?"

"You could save some and your future husband could save some too. It's the least he could do if he wants you."

"The least he could do?" Teresina mused. That's what everyone had done for her—the least they could. She stood up and started pacing around the small room. "We'll see," she murmured. "We'll see, but now I have to kill the goat so I don't have to pay the tax on it. This government can think of more things to tax. First they kept the tax on bread. Now they're taxing goats. Don't they know how much we depend on goats? Now we won't have their milk to make cheese. Luigi, come help me. We need to kill the goat," she called.

Luigi came in from collecting capers growing on the rocks. He placed the basket holding them onto the kitchen table. How he loved when his mother marinated them in vinegar and then used them in her tomato sauce. A gentle boy, he didn't look forward to this latest chore, but it had to be done and if done correctly, it could be accomplished with a minimum of upset.

I imagine him going outside to put a rope around the goat's neck and quickly tying its front legs together and doing the same to her back legs. Concetta looks on. She turns the goat on her back while Teresina sharpens her knife. The goat bleats as if she knew what was going to happen. Then Teresina picks up a pail and grabs the goat by the rope around its neck. She places the pail on the ground by the goat's neck and then slits her throat. She catches the goat's blood in the pail so she can make blood sausage out of it.

A man comes strolling down the road. His black shoes are covered with dust and he carries his jacket over his shoulders. "Why are you killing your goat, Signora?" he asks.

"Because the government taxes goats. I'd rather eat it than pay taxes—not that I have the money. We don't get any benefit from the taxes we pay the government. Nothing's changed since the revolution."

"Do you mean since Garibaldi and his troops united Italy and drove the foreigners out?"

"All I know is that nothing's changed for us. Who cares about the government? The only change I see is for the worse. The Church's communal lands were divided up. Now we can't forage for dead wood for our fires. We're digging up roots to burn. And we can't forage for mushrooms the way we use to or__."

"Ah yes, I've heard about these problems and more. How a German company came and cut down all the trees near here for lumber and now the topsoil washes away with every little rain."

"Yes, and then the rivers overflow," she says. "But you must be thirsty. Come in out of the sun and I'll give you a glass of water." She sends Rosa for the water jug half buried in the ground to keep it cool. Concetta and Luigi follow her and the stranger inside.

"Ah, this water has a strong sulphuric taste, Signore,"

"Yes, it comes from the fountain in the center of town. They're healing waters."

"I see." When he finishes drinking, he tells her he is traveling to Sibari, the ancient Greek town.

"Greek," repeats Teresina. She knows about that language. She refers to the people in the next town as the people who speak Greek. She tells the man that.

"Do you know any Greek?" he asks.

"I don't know," Teresina shrugs.

"What's your word for this?" he points to an eggplant lying on the table.

"Moolinjian," Teresina answers.

"That's a variation on a Greek word," he smiles and takes out his notebook. He writes in it. The women's eyes follow his hand as he writes. He points to some beans in a bowl.

"That's fazool," she says.

"H-m, I'm not sure if that's Greek. It sounds more like it comes from Arabic."

He asks her some more words and these he tells her are from the ancient Greek.

"Where are you from?"

"From France," he replies.

"Where is that?" I imagine my grandmother asking him, just as the peasant woman in Douglas's book asks Douglas where England is. Like that other peasant woman my grandmother's had no education and she predates the mass media as well so that she has no means of learning about the world around her. When, as an adult, I tell her that I'd be living in France for a year, she asks me where this France is. It's only then that I realize she's had no way of knowing of its existence.

"North of here," I have the man reply.

"And do they speak Greek over there?" wonders Teresina.

"No, no," he answers. "They speak French."

"And what does French sound like?"

"Like this," and he says a sentence or two in French.

"No-o," Teresina said. "Do people really talk like that?"

The man smiles and assures her that they do.

"And they understand this strange language?" she muses.

"Why, yes, they do. It's their language, just as Italian is yours."

"I see what you mean...you're certainly adventurous. Aren't you afraid of the brigands?"

"Oh, there are none in this area. Brigands hide out

south of here in the Sila Mountains. I'll be fine."

"Best to be careful."

The sun begins to sink in the sky. The air starts to cool. The man bids farewell to the two women and the children.

"I'm going into town to meet a coachman who will drive me to Sibari. That was a Greek city many years ago—in ancient times. That why some of your words are still from the ancient Greek. Ancient Sybari was a very rich city with people who knew how to live well."

"Ah, Signore, we all know how to live well, but we need work in order to do that. What sort of work did these Sibarites do to get so rich? Did they go to America?"

"No, no," the man laughs. "They knew nothing of America. They were rich long before Cristiforo Colombo discovered America. They had a great trading port plus their people were known for their metal work. And two rivers surrounded the city and gave it fertile soil."

"Ah, not like our land. Even when the men were still here to farm it, it was parched and dry. And then when the rains finally come, they come in a flood and ruin the crops. It's no wonder all the men go to America."

"And is that where your husband is?"

"Concetta's husband is in America, but..." she lowers her eyes, "...mine is dead."

"I'm sorry to hear that, Signora." He offers her his hand and turns to leave.

"But my sister here is telling me about a man in America who wants to marry me, a woman with three children. What do you think of that?"

"Italy is a hard land for a widow, and America is not easy either. But it might offer hope to your children."

"They're who I live for, Signore. Maybe I'll see you there some day."

"Maybe," he says. "Good luck, Signora."

The man continues on his way. Teresina looks after him, mulling over what he's said. She thinks about her life in Italy. The tax on the salt she needs to preserve the goat meat has increased by a factor of five. She sighs. As the sun sinks, Teresina continues to stare down the road, wondering what's in store for her. Should she marry this stranger in America who was Michele's relative? He must be a good man—all Michele's relatives were responsible people. Yet none of them helped her. No one could help her. Here no one had anything extra to share with her or offer her. Imagine having to raise the money to go to America. It was an enormous sum, but many people in America saved enough dollars to send for their relatives.

Four years later the man who was to become Teresina's second husband sent her some of the money for passage on the ship that was to take them to America. Teresina supplied the rest through her constant frugality. Concetta and her husband, who was back for his yearly visit, accompanied Teresina and her children to the ship. Their leaving was poignant. Like many of the immigrants, those leaving and those staying held onto either end of a long piece of yarn, Concetta and her husband on the pier and Teresina on the deck. As the ship left the pier, streamers of different colored yarns swayed and stretched from ship to shore until no more yarn was left. Teresina reluctantly let the yarn go. The connection was severed and the yarn blew away in the breeze.

Rosa loved the ship and skipped about all over while Michelina, now four, thought she was going to die from seasickness. When the four of them landed at Ellis Island, they got in various lines with all the other immigrants. Given the situation, things proceeded well enough until it was time for the physical evaluation. Luigi's jacket was marked with an X and he was moved to a different line from his mother and sisters.

"What's happening?" Teresina started shouting as two men moved Luigi away from her. She went to grab him but the men barred her with their arms from touching her son.

With her arms extended, she called out to Luigi. "*Figlio mio,* come back, come back." A matron slid beside her and led her and the two girls to an interpreter. The interpreter explained that her son was being detained because of his eyes. He seemed to have a disease that was common among immigrants, and he had to be examined further. Teresina furrowed her brow. They waited to hear what the verdict was.

"Signore," the matron began, "Your son does have an eye disease that prohibits him from entering the United States. He will be returned to Italy."

The girls began to cry. "What am I going to do?" Teresina yelled. "My son, my son," she sobbed. The matron took the family aside.

"Your son will be allowed to enter once his eyes are healed. You have to decide if you want to stay here in America or return with him."

It was no decision for Teresina to make. It had taken four years of savings by her and her future husband to get them here. She couldn't go back. She brushed away her tears and, with the two girls straggling behind her, moved forward to meet her future husband.

Standing before her was a good-looking man in rumpled and dirty clothing, accompanied by three children. The two boys looked like their father. The girl was very skinny. The three seemed to be about the same age as her children. The man stood with a pea cap squashed between his hands. "Teresina, I'm to be your husband. These are my children, Jesse, Dan, and Angelina." All six children stared at each other. Then Teresina smiled at the children. They smiled back.

"Let's go," their father commanded. "I have to get back to work." He picked up some of Teresina's belongings. His children turned and hurried along beside him. Teresina and her children followed, carrying the rest of their valises as best they could.

The tenement on Thompson Street above Houston was small and dark. Teresina was married now and her husband was the superintendent of the building. Besides stoking the furnace, he was responsible for keeping the hallways and stairs clean as well as doing minor repairs. He made it clear to Teresina that she would have to support her own children. A neighbor woman took her to the clothing factory she worked in to see about a job.

Teresina was getting used to the tall buildings that made up this city of Nuova York. But she wasn't prepared for the factory. Seeing so many women sewing on machines startled her. The boss led her with the neighbor woman tagging along as interpreter to a large pressing machine.

"I fired the guy who worked here—a lazy son-of-a-gun. This is a man's job, but she can have it if she wants it— three dollars a week. I'll show her how to use the machine to press the suits we make." The neighbor translated.

Three dollars a week. So much money amazed Teresina. "I can do it," Teresina said. "I'm very strong." And do it she did, even in the hot summer months when the steam from the pressing machine enveloped her upper body. She felt proud to be doing a man's job and it was a source of pride to her children too.

Michelina was enrolled at public school. She spoke no English until she arrived there and so her fellow Italian classmates referred to her as the greenhorn. They laughed at her name when her teacher called the roll. Perhaps this was when she began thinking about Americanizing her first name and Frenchifying her last by changing the ending in Guerrieri from an 'i' to an 'e.'

When Teresina quickly learned that three dollars a week did not go far in America, she took in laundry to wash at night. On Sundays when she took out her children for ice cream, she invited her husband's three even though he never reciprocated. If there was money to buy ice cream, he bought it only for his children. Her marriage was a huge disappointment. Not only was her husband niggardly with her children, he was an abusive alcoholic, who insisted they all eat supper with him in the basement furnace room. After supper in that dreadful room, Michelina and Rosa sat in straight-backed chairs to be sure their stepfather would not abuse their mother. But like it or not, he was her husband and Teresina knew she would have to endure. Since the death of her first husband and even before that, her life had been about endurance. She had worked in the fields as a child with no opportunity to attend school. She had even endured the separation from her son for three long years.

By 1910, Teresina had saved enough money to return with her two daughters to Italy. Once again they boarded a boat but this time it was going *to* Italy. They heard the ship's bell clang as it got underway. Steam puffed from its chimney and after a long, tiring voyage, they arrived in Naples.

Luigi couldn't wait to see them. He had traveled to Naples to meet his family. At age fourteen, he was considered a man. He had spent his time in Italy learning two trades, barbering and tailoring.

Years later when I visited an exclusive British-owned hotel and restaurant on Calabria's west coast, I tried to put the young boy who was our waiter's assistant at ease by chatting with him. A tall, good-looking boy, he was thirteen years old, he told me. I asked if he was working there on school vacation. No, he told me, he no longer went to school. He was apprenticing for this job as waiter.

I was shocked. This was the nineteen sixties. I naively thought that such occurrences were a thing of the past. I thought back to a scene I had seen a week earlier on our way to the hotel: a boy of about eleven wearing dusty overalls carried a large piece of wood on his shoulder. A man I assumed was his father, also in grimy overalls, walked behind. But perhaps the real story was that this young boy was also apprenticed out, in this situation to a carpenter. This culture still didn't have the luxury of childhood as a concept.

Luigi's eyes had healed. He looked for his mother and sisters among the crowd of people lining the ship's railing. He spotted them right away, but his mother was still searching the milling crowd on the dock for her little Luigini. He had been only eleven, a boy, when they left. Now he was a six-foot tall man, dressed in a dark suit he had made himself, a dapper hat on his curly hair.

Luigi waved up to his mother and sisters over the heads of the people on the dock waiting for their relatives' return. His mother continued to search the faces in the crowd. Her brow furrowed. The passengers began to disembark. She still had not seen Luigi. And then she recognized him, her Luigi. She dropped the hands of her daughters and rushed towards him, singing his name between sobs, pushing aside those people who were slow in making way for her reunion with her son.

She stood there crying in his arms. Rosa and Michelina slowly made their way forward and joined in the hugging. Luigi looked down at them and smiled. No further words were needed as they made their way back to Lauropoli.

They stayed almost a year, long enough for Teresina to assess the situation. Would it be better to stay in Italy or return to America? Although Luigi was working as a tailor, few customers were to be had in their small town. No middle class existed for such services. With families separated, half in Italy and half in America, it was harder than ever to raise a decent crop. Teresina saw no future in running a gristmill. She observed that while immigration had helped some of the Italians who remained in Italy—a scarcity of workers had driven up wages—her situation hadn't improved.

In 1911 the family boarded the *Ancona* in Naples and returned to America. On the ship's manifest, Teresina's last name is garbled and Michelina is listed as four years old instead of eight. Due to malnourishment, she could perhaps be mistaken for four. She and her family had continued to eat as they had done in Italy with lots of bread but little meat or other protein. Mistakes on manifests were common and nothing was made of it. They were back in America.

Six years later, Michelina graduated from eighth grade. She went to work on Eighth Street at a candy factory, boxing chocolates. She said it was a cleaner job than working in a factory. So many of them blew dirt and dust all around you and the noise was deafening. At night with her relative Elsie, she attended secretarial school in Brooklyn for two years and through her, she landed a job as a secretary at Reo Cars. She loved the job, but felt shy in this new environment. Her boss's wife thought she was so pretty that she moved her up to the front of the office.

Although Luigi became a citizen in 1919, Margaret, as she now called herself, waited until 1927 to become one. Why she waited so long, I don't know, nor do I know why she finally started the process. Perhaps the Sacco and Vanzetti case that ran from 1920 to 1927 was the impetus. Perhaps it had to do with nativism growing due to the Red Scare after the Russian Revolution and the resultant Palmer Raids of 1919 and 1920. Or maybe it was the restrictive immigration laws passed in 1924; perhaps she thought it wise to become a citizen while she still could.

She became close to the wife of her boss at Reo cars, a

family-run business. When she married in 1934, the woman wrote my mother a beautiful letter, which she saved until she died, when I discovered it. She had never shown it to any of us. It read:

Dear Mrs. Bonomo,

Does it sound natural yet? But (sic) always Margaret to us you know.

I want to again tell you what a wonderful time we had at your wedding party, it was absolutely perfect in every respect. Please once more thank your mother for including us among your guests.

You know they say at a wedding one always tells the bride all the lovely things and the poor groom stands by and nobody ever tell him he is nice. So I want to say your husband looked very nice and I surely congratulate him as a perfect host and after last eve, you need never worry about him being able to do his part as head of your home.

I hope you both will have a very, very delightful trip and not only have a good time, but rest. I am sure the whole thing has been quite a strain upon you both. When you return to your own home and start on the pathway of your life together you must be rested and fit to meet life before you.

I want to thank you Margaret for all the years of faithfulness you have given Mr. Stone. You would be that to anybody, but you have no idea all it means to a business man, to have associated with him one he can always trust and to a wife who shares his joys and his troubles, that kind of a person becomes very dear and so Margaret I have truly learned to love you dear.

In the years to come you both will look back with such joy to your beautiful wedding and I know a happy honey-moon—A message of love to your mother and a heartful of it to you and your husband—

Mrs. George/Carol Pike Stone

October, twenty-nine—1934

P. S. a neighbor tells me Bonomo, means "a good man," I think that is a fine, am sure he is even if it is not a correct definition of it. CPS

Mrs. Salvator Bonomo

173 Sullivan Street

City of New York

I would not be at all surprised if I was Carol Stone's namesake since my mother was always on the lookout for 'American' names, but I'll never know since when my mother was alive she didn't mention whom I was named after.

Reo Cars would indirectly play a part in our lives. Years later my father helped his brother out of a financial jam. Quite a bit older than my father, his brother Mike had become a secretary to a stockbroker. Though he had been born in Italy in 1881, he was the most Americanized of any of my relatives. He was slim and well-spoken, two characteristics which I associated with being American.

My brother and I saw him in the 1940s until he died in 1948. We never visited him at his house. He always came to our house for dinner, dressed in a dark suit. Though well made, it was old and out of date and gave off an air of genteel poverty.

According to my father, my Uncle Mike had made and lost three fortunes. My father explained that, in those days, $75,000 constituted a fortune. Like everyone else during the roaring twenties, my uncle bought stock on margin. A few years after the stock market collapsed, he needed money to pay off his stock buying debts.

He and my father, who was now courting my mother, sat down to look at my father's portfolio to see which stocks he would sell off to raise cash for my uncle. My father had learned about stocks from Mike, who had taught my father what he knew. My father was a careful investor who would read the stock's prospectus as well as the business pages of the newspapers, and rarely, if ever, did he buy on margin.

They weighed the pros and cons of selling this stock and that stock. They considered each one's value and future growth. They discussed what they each knew about the list of stocks. One of the stocks they considered selling was Reo cars, which my father had bought because of my mother's working at the company. They weighed its merits along with the merits of other stocks. They rejected selling Reo cars perhaps because of the personal connection to the company. Finally my father and uncle decided to sell my father's shares of General Motors. Whenever my father told this story, he told it as the biggest joke on him. There was never a hint of regret or bitterness about having sold the stock to help his brother—even if it meant he wouldn't become a millionaire.

Unlike his brother Mike, my father never aspired to be rich. When Mike was in the chips, as my mother told me, he was a big spender, taking trips to Paris with his girl friend and buying many costly items. When he died, we inherited a lovely Parisian clock that chimed the hours and half hours.

My father wanted to be comfortable, certainly, but he had no use for great wealth or perhaps no imagination for it. Once when I was older and the newspapers reported on Elvis Presley's solid gold Cadillac, he maintained, "That's the cause of Communism." What he meant was that that kind of disparity in people's fortunes in a country, where poverty existed, could give rise to great dissatisfaction and result in sufficient unrest to cause Communism.

Meanwhile my mother's sister, who now called herself Rose, had married Frank Grande in 1914. They had one child, Angela. My mother adored her brother-in-law and he became a father substitute for her. The young family bought a house on Staten Island but during the flu epidemic of 1918 Frank had succumbed to the sickness.

Now a widow my aunt lost the house. Rose went to work at Rogers Peet Company, sewing in the linings to men's suits and coats. Angela, whom everyone called Lillie in one of those practices of name changing that so many immigrants favored, eventually joined her mother in the same factory.

Rose remarried a man, whom I always thought of as a charlatan, and had a son by him. I never saw Uncle Charlie work a day in his life, but he seemed to have a little bit of money to spend. He spent his time doing medical drawings and writing, in a very small, fine hand, about the body. His interest in the body almost seemed lurid to me so that I determined by age twelve that it was best if I never visited at a time when my aunt and her daughter were not at home.

His 'fine' handwriting alone would be sufficient to convince some neighbors that he was an educated man. His ability to speak 'standard' Italian was another skill that would impress them. And he spoke authoritatively on any subject. I had seen him go into minor rages when his son contradicted him in even a small way. My uncle rarely wore a shirt so that his stomach, as big and hard as a medicine ball, often seemed like a wall of steel that you didn't want to tangle with out of fear of being obliterated by it.

No book was ever published, but neighbors seemed to respect him as an educated man or as a doctor of mental problems—perhaps of a folk culture medical type of shaman or one who lays on of hands. I could envision his authoritatively laying on of hands and commanding someone to be cured since he always spoke in a robust and imposing manner, dripping with 'humble' superiority as he attempted to educate you to *his* opinions.

When I went to the hospital to visit him in his final illness, I was shocked by how weak he was. As I was leaving, my aunt and her daughter, both near tears and full of concern for my Uncle Charlie, hovered over me, my aunt's stoop exaggerated by her worry. They asked how he looked to me. I was so struck by their all too evident anxiety for this man whom I felt had given my aunt and her daughter nothing but his posturing. Yet I too was touched by his condition and tears filled my eyes. Not wanting to worry them, I made some noncommittal remark, which I thought was what they wanted to hear. Love, I thought, is not to be explained nor was what I viewed as my aunt's and her daughter's saintliness in caring for this man to the very end, to be explained.

The family lived in a four-room tenement opposite St. Anthony of Padua Church. The front door of their walk-up opened right into the kitchen. A huge room with a large window looking out onto Houston Street and letting in lots of light, it was the center of daily life. When we visited, we first sat around the kitchen table. A bedroom was situated off the kitchen and another one off the adjoining living room. The bathroom was tucked away to the side of the kitchen. I always disliked having to use that bathroom because it was cold and heated by a little gas stove that scared me. Everyone was afraid that it would tip over and start a fire.

But no fire ever started and my extended family continued not only to make their way in their new country but also to thrive. I married, had two children, lived in France for two years and in Italy for two months, and attended Bread Loaf Writers Conference and graduate school at Brown University. I taught Puerto Rican students in the South Bronx, black students in the Dixwell neighborhood of New Haven, at a private school in Providence, at the University of Rhode Island and Harvard University Extension School, made educational videotapes while employed at the Rhode Island Department of Environmental Management.

When I worked as a curriculum designer at Brown University's Medical School, I developed a unit of study, using scenes from plays to teach psychosocial issues of medicine. In my spare time, I appeared in plays at Providence's Barker Players (my role as Sally, a Southern belle in *Auntie Mame* was my favorite), joined both a Summer Chorus and an Italian *Coro,* took up pottery, and ran unsuccessfully for the Rhode Island state senate against the minority leader.

Almost all the extended family's children of my generation attended college and some attended graduate school and became professionals. Unlike our ancestors, we had vocational choices we could act on and opportunities to individuate and follow our interests. While trying to solve the confusion of two identities, we experienced the promise of America, which included the pursuit of happiness. We didn't always succeed in achieving this delicate balance of identities but somehow we flourished in the resultant stew and even retained our interest in things Italian. It's now up to the next generation, far removed from those original courageous immigrants, to carry on in the face of new challenges.

Italians are big into fate. My mother always talked about it while I, rolling my eyes, remained dubious. My feelings about fate coincide more with Leonard Woolf's. He wrote that "You cannot escape Fate and Fate, I have always felt, is not in the future, but in the past." And so I have written this memoir for my grandchildren that they may have knowledge of their fate.